PLANNING ANIMATION

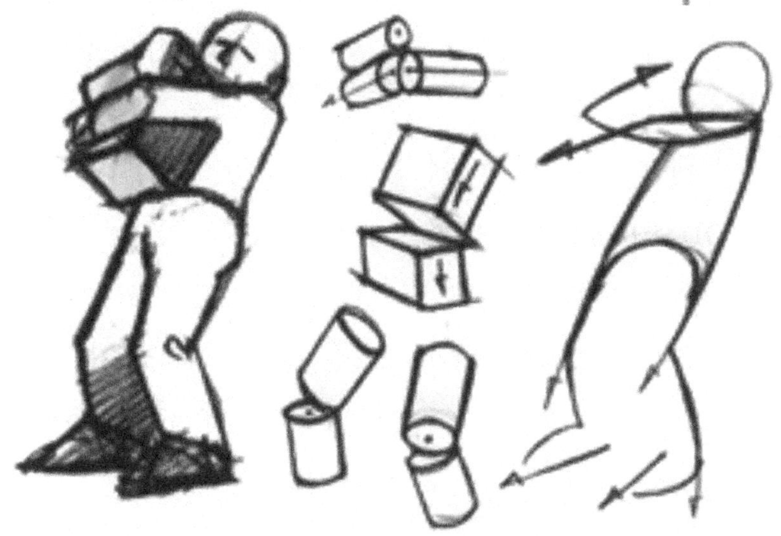

Anamie Entertainment Ltd.
ISBN: 978-0-9713439-0-0

Dedicated to those who discover.

 # Simplified Drawing for Planning

If you animate in 2D, 3D, stop motion or cuts outs; if you illustrate, cartoon or design characters, the fastest way to plan is with simple, informative, sketches.

The sections of the book are presented in reverse order. The goal is first, how to get there starts at the end. Read the book front to back then do the exercises from back to front.

Learn to short hand your drawings. Focus on communicating the idea behind the drawing, the reason for the movement in your animation, the story in your illustration, the character, the action and emotion.

Get reference, make decisions, know what you want to create, then explore. Make music with controlled, simplified drawings.

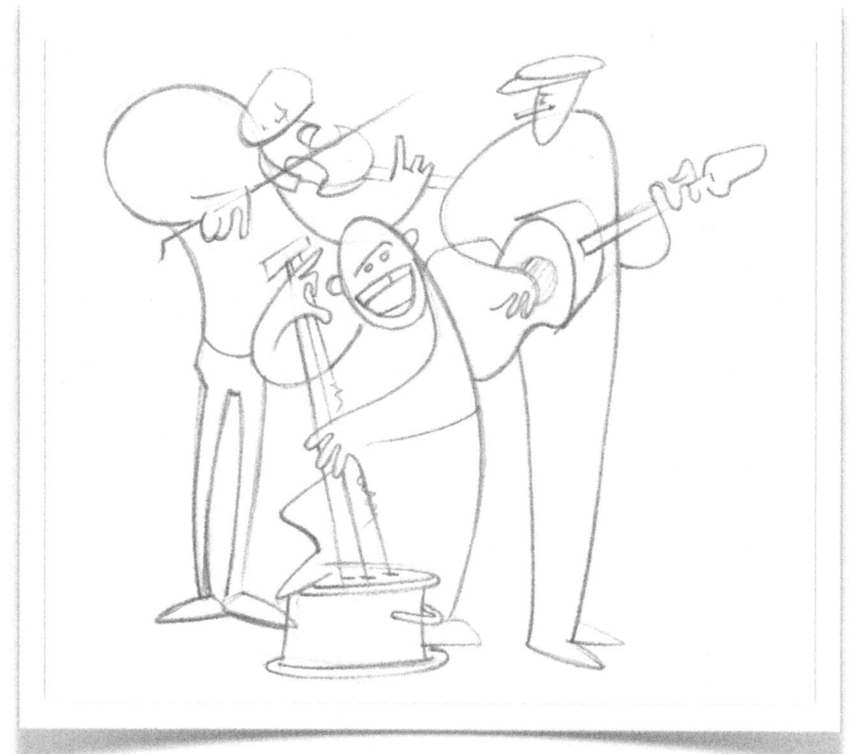

The more planning you do the faster you will finish and the results will be far more impressive.

The more you know about the subject's structure, the easier it is to simplify your drawings. This shorthand drawing based on knowledge also applies to animals, creatures and landscapes; it enhances your life drawing, comic art and illustration skills.

Mastering drawing skills is a life long adventure. The information in this book is focused mostly on simplified human body structure which allows you to interpret subject matter through poses that capture the essence of what you wish to communicate.

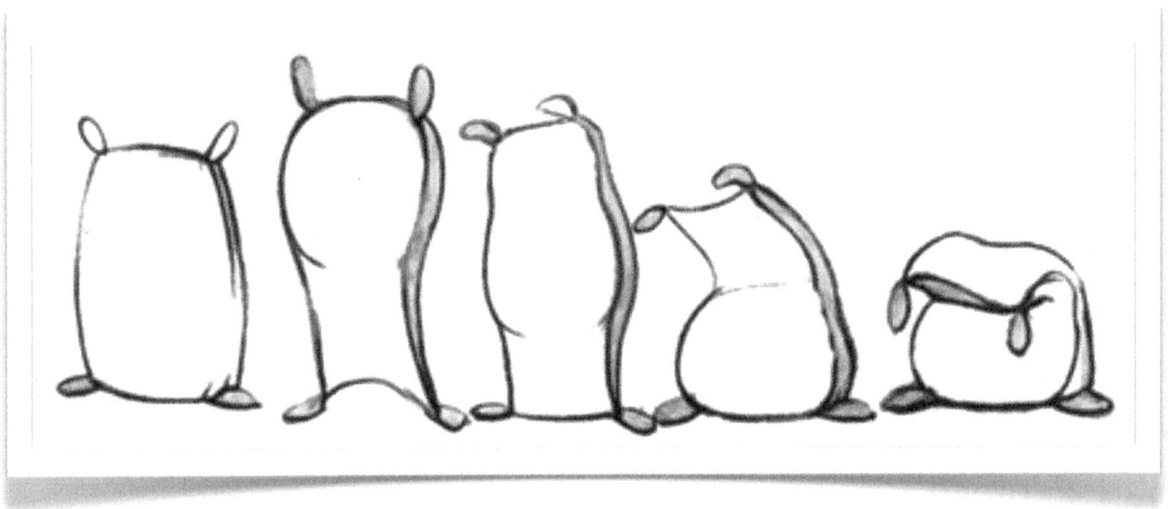

Every person stands in a unique way. Posture describes character and emotional state. Does your character have a straight back, squared or slouched shoulders, are they knock kneed or pigeon toed? Use the structural information in this book as a foundation for communicating with your drawings.

POSING YOUR CHARACTER

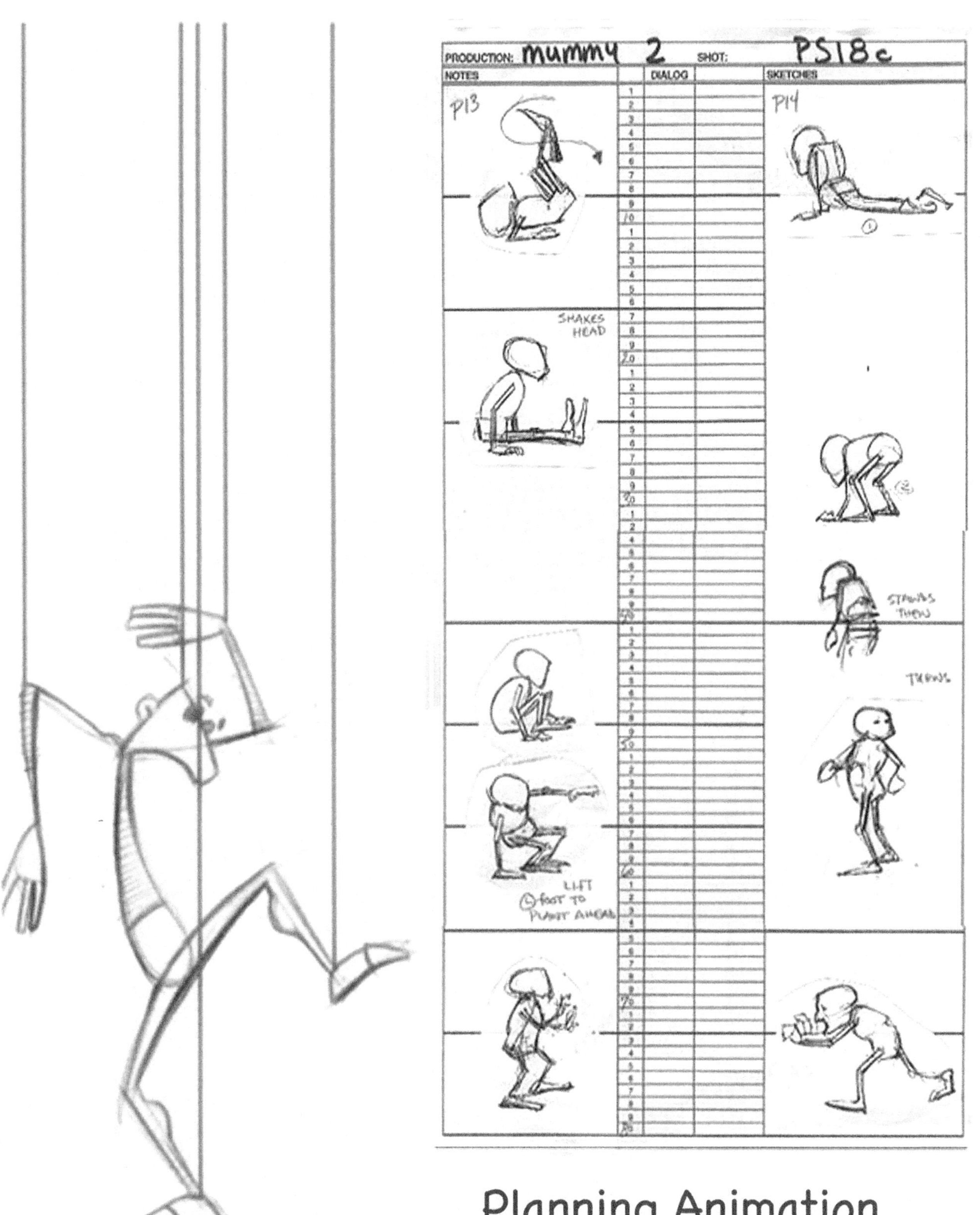

Planning Animation

DESIGN THE ESSENCE OF THE CHARACTER

START WITH 3 LINES - 2 SIDES, SHOULDERS AND A HEAD SHAPE.
ALTER THESE LINES UNTIL YOU HAVE THE DESIGN THAT YOU WANT.

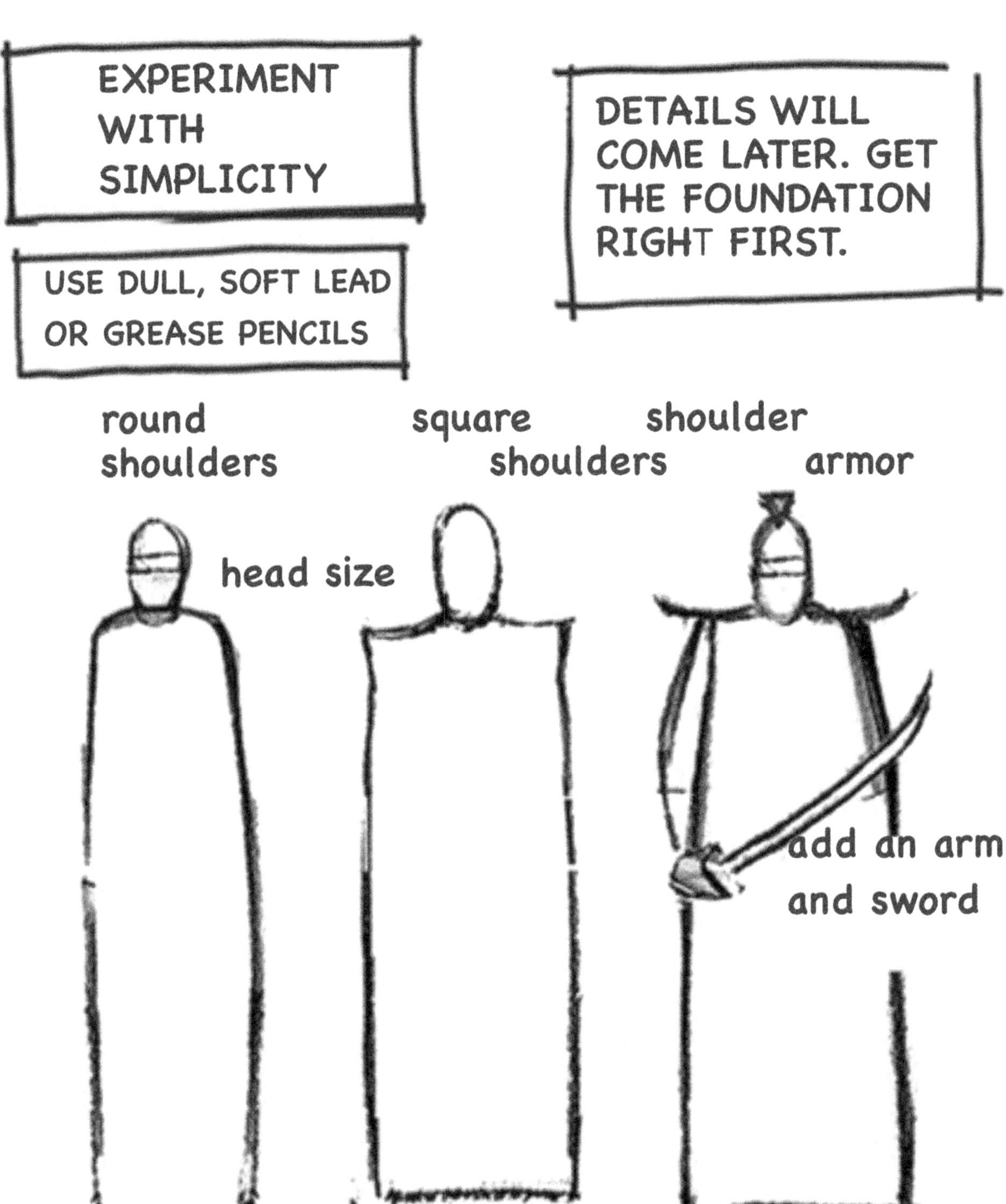

KEEP IT AS SIMPLE AS POSSIBLE

DESIGN THE ESSENCE OF THE CHARACTER

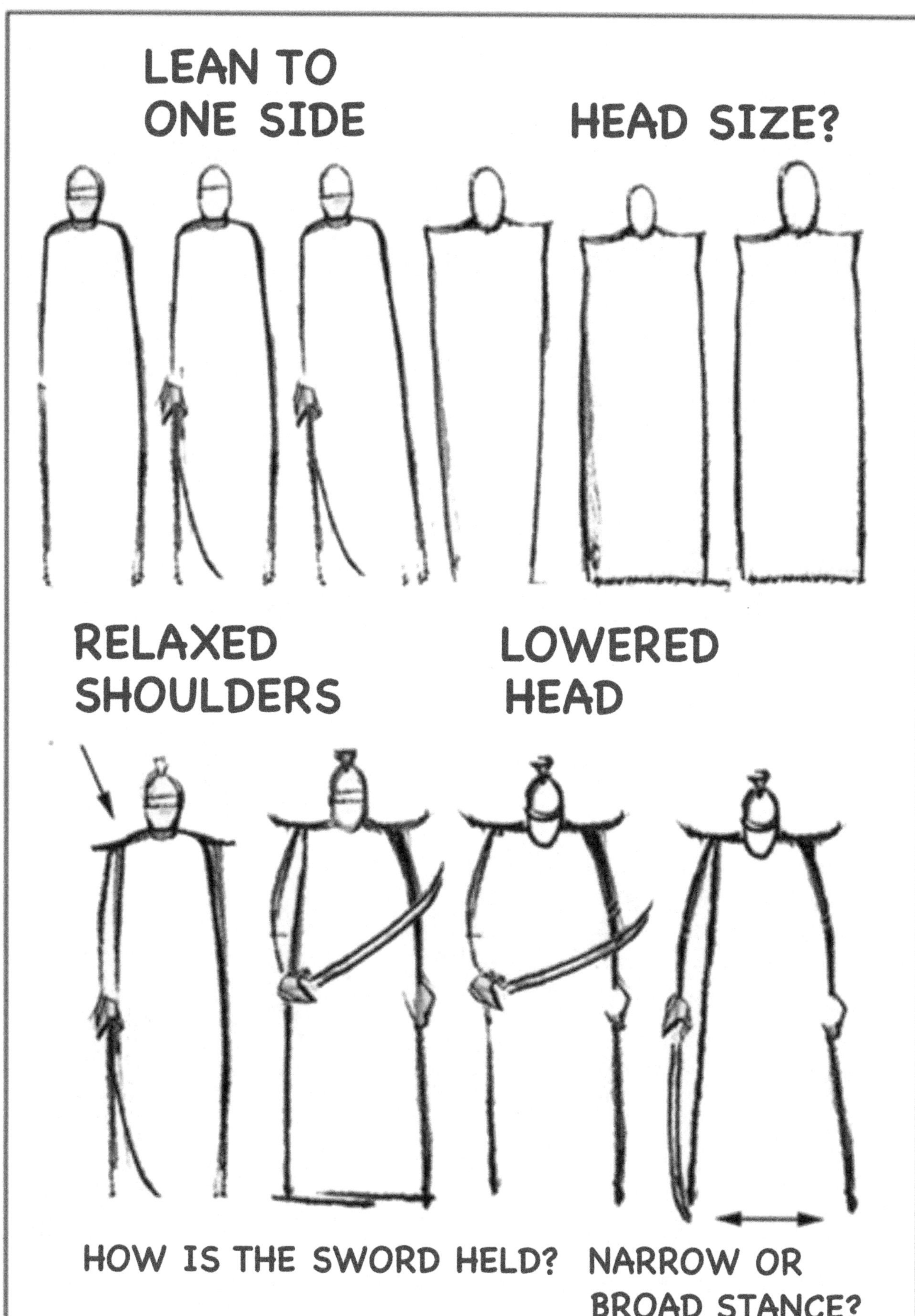

POSE AND POSTURE

A character comes to you as a 2D model sheet, a 3D default pose, a stop motion puppet, an asset in Flash or Harmony. Your first task is to pose the character in a way that describes personality, emotion, energy and represents the story behind the image.

WHAT MAKES A STRONG POSE?

A good pose clearly describes the action and acting you wish to convey. It describes forces that have influenced the character. The term 'force' is emphasized in animation because without it there would not be movement. Action and acting are the two forms of force to focus on. Action is possibly the easiest to show in your drawings and animation. It is shown through external movement such as pulling, pushing, lifting, hitting, throwing, jumping, climbing...

Some passive actions are sitting, standing, kneeling and lying down. They are the start and end poses of an action and must show character personality and emotion. Acting is an internal force. It shows how the character feels and that they are thinking. When you decide what the character's personality and emotional state are: energetic, lazy, brave, cowardly, angry, excited, sad...

INTERNAL AND EXTERNAL FORCES DICTATE A CHARACTER'S POSTURE AND MOVEMENT

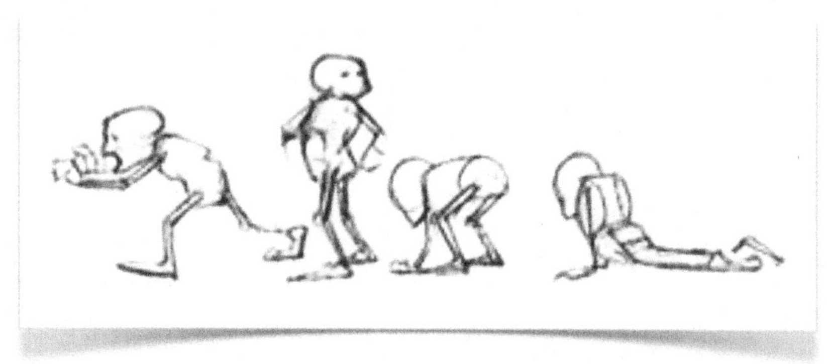

DESIGN AND POSING BEFORE ANIMATING

Let's animate a short film about boxing. First comes research. Go to a boxing match with a video camera and sketch book, go to the library, watch films, start a fight, no, wait, let that one go.

Do a series of design sketches to create the characters you will animate. Start with the previous exercise using basic shapes and simple lines.

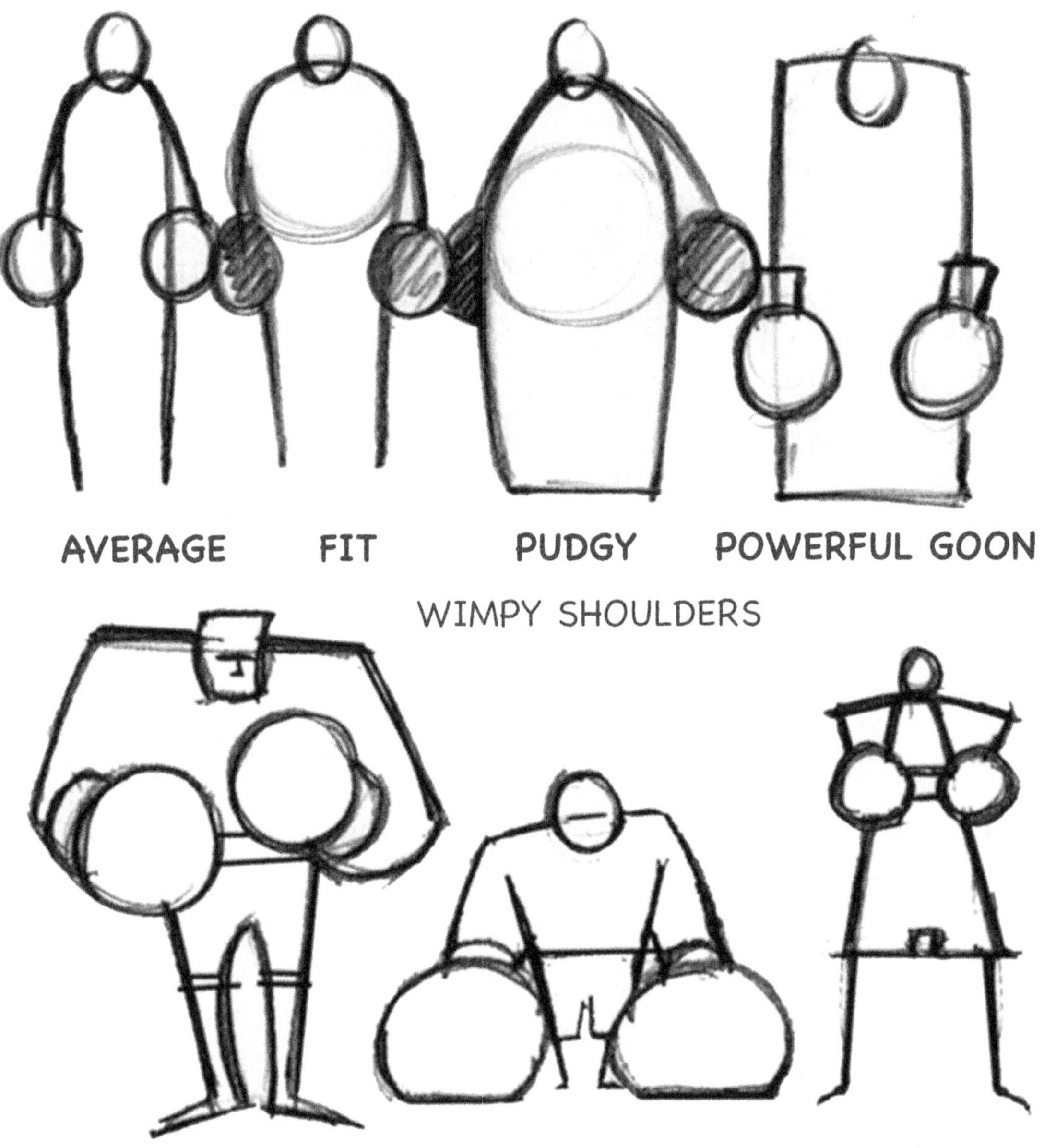

DO 2 OR 3 PAGES OF SIMPLE DESIGN SKETCHES FOR BASEBALL, GOLF, HOCKEY, BASKETBALL...

POSING

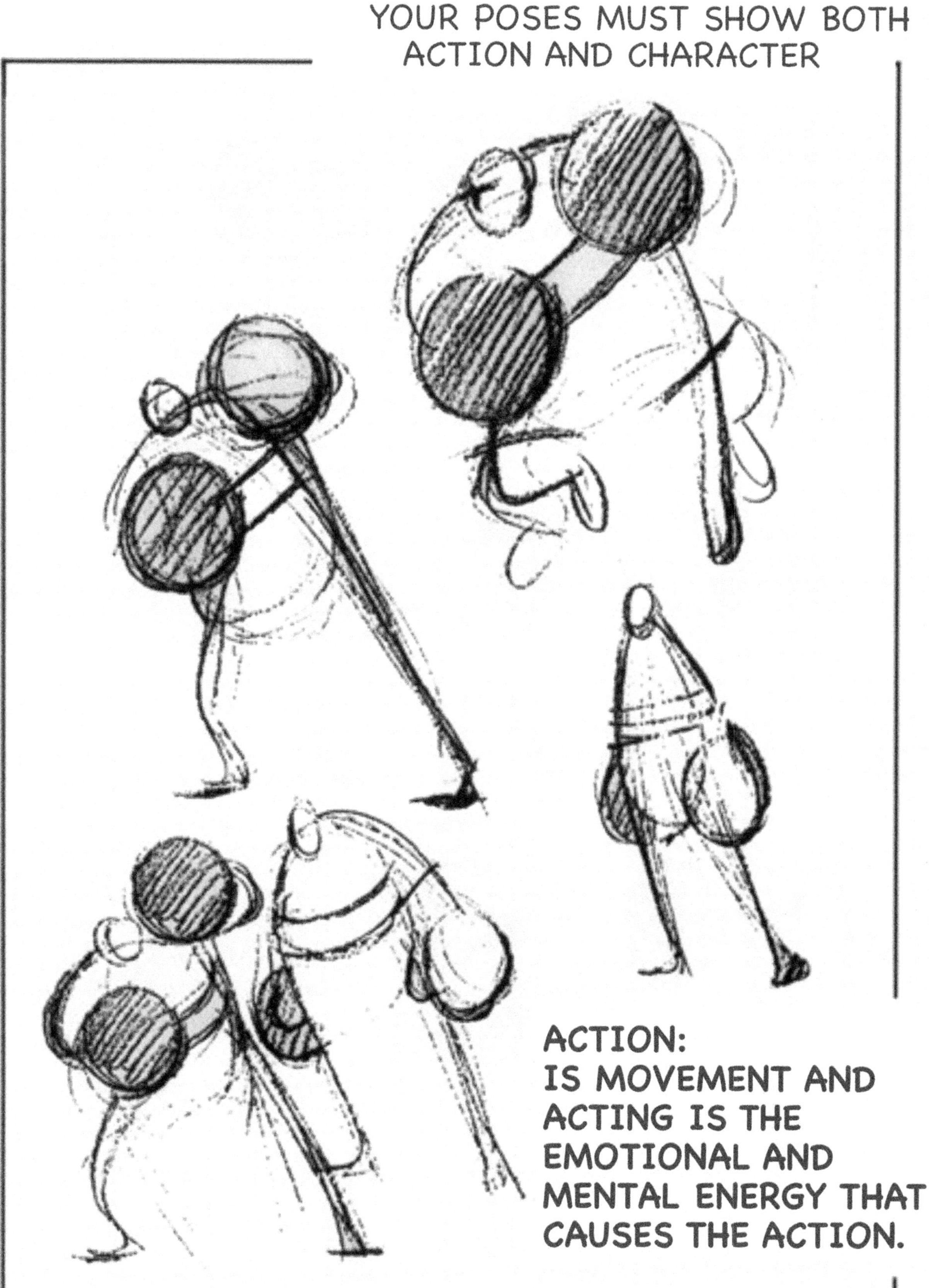

ACTION:
IS MOVEMENT AND
ACTING IS THE
EMOTIONAL AND
MENTAL ENERGY THAT
CAUSES THE ACTION.

DRAW AS MANY ACTING AND ACTION POSE AS YOU CAN IN 1 HOUR

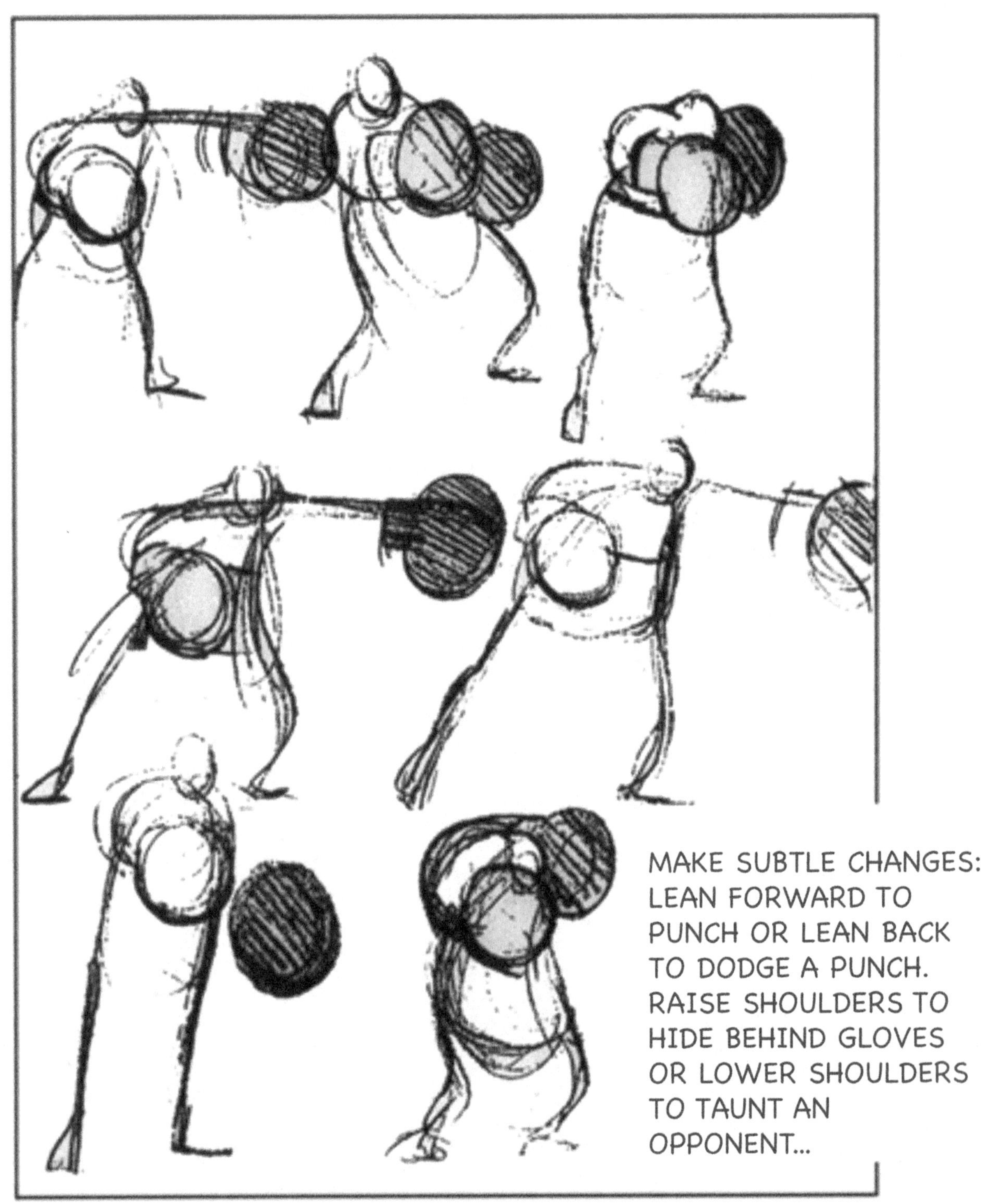

THE THOUGHTS THAT GO ON IN A BOXER'S HEAD ARE THE FORCES OR REASONS FOR THE ACTIONS AND POSES. CAPTURE THE REASONS FOR THE POSES WHEN YOU DRAW.

POSING

Choose a number of sports and create characters through poses.

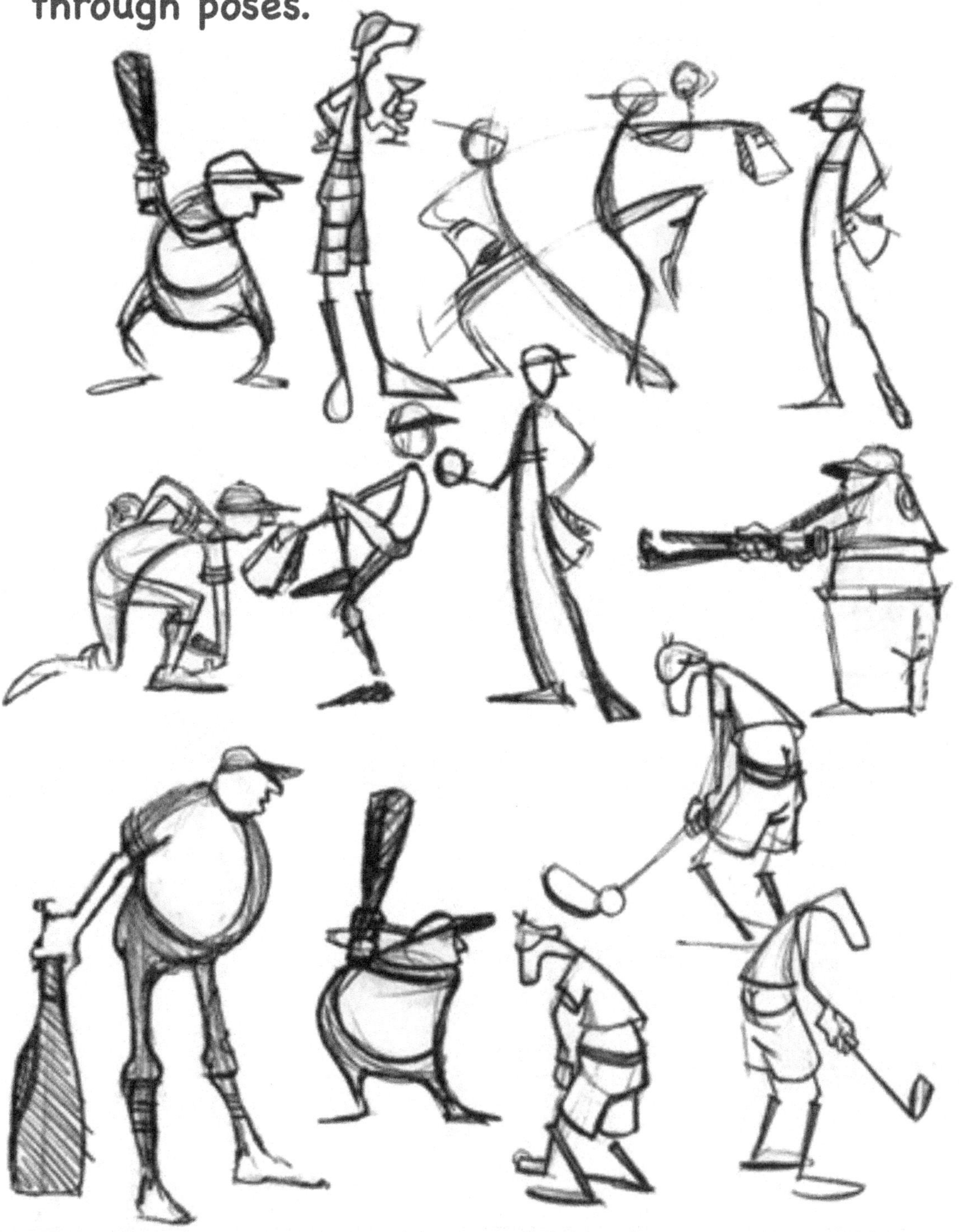

CAPTURE IN YOUR DRAWINGS AND ANIMATION THE REASON
BEHIND THE ACTION. WHAT IS THE PITCHER THINKING
BEFORE THE PITCH? ... THE BATTER BEFORE THE PITCH? LET
THEIR THOUGHTS CREATE POSES - BODY LANGUAGE

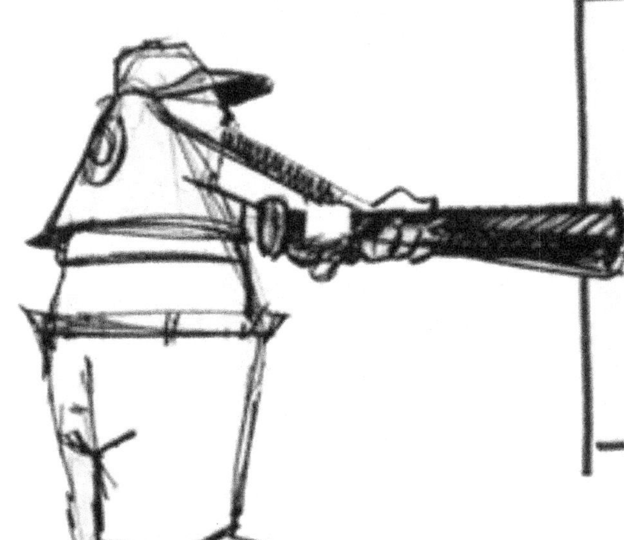

THE BODY CAN BE BROKEN DOWN INTO A FEW SIMPLE GEOMETRIC SHAPES. THESE SHAPES ARE CONNECTED TO ONE ANOTHER AND ALLOW MOVEMENT. POSTURE IS CREATED BY THE ALIGNMENT OF THESE SHAPES. POSTURE SHOWS ATTITUDE - THE INNER ESSENCE OF A CHARACTER.

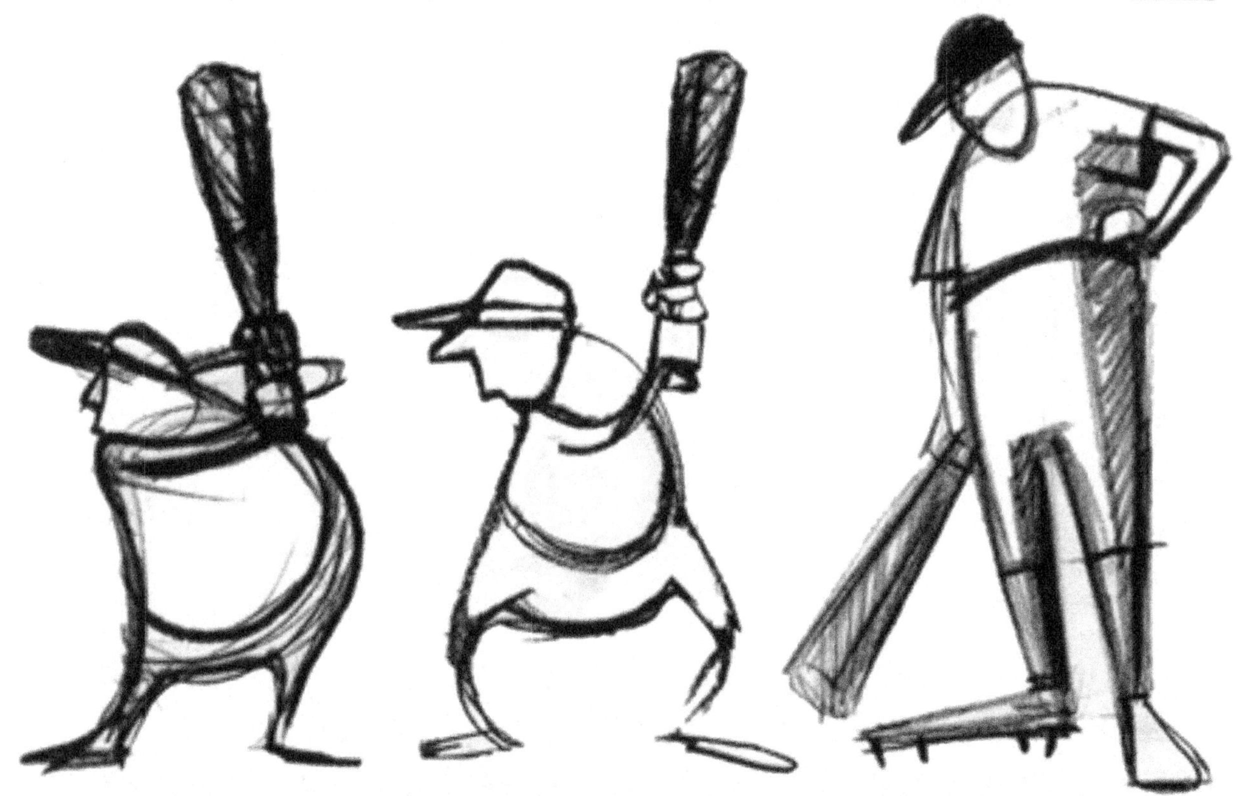

SUBTLE RE-ALIGNMENT OF THESE BODY PARTS CAN DRASTICALLY CHANGE OUR CHARACTER'S VISUAL ATTITUDE.

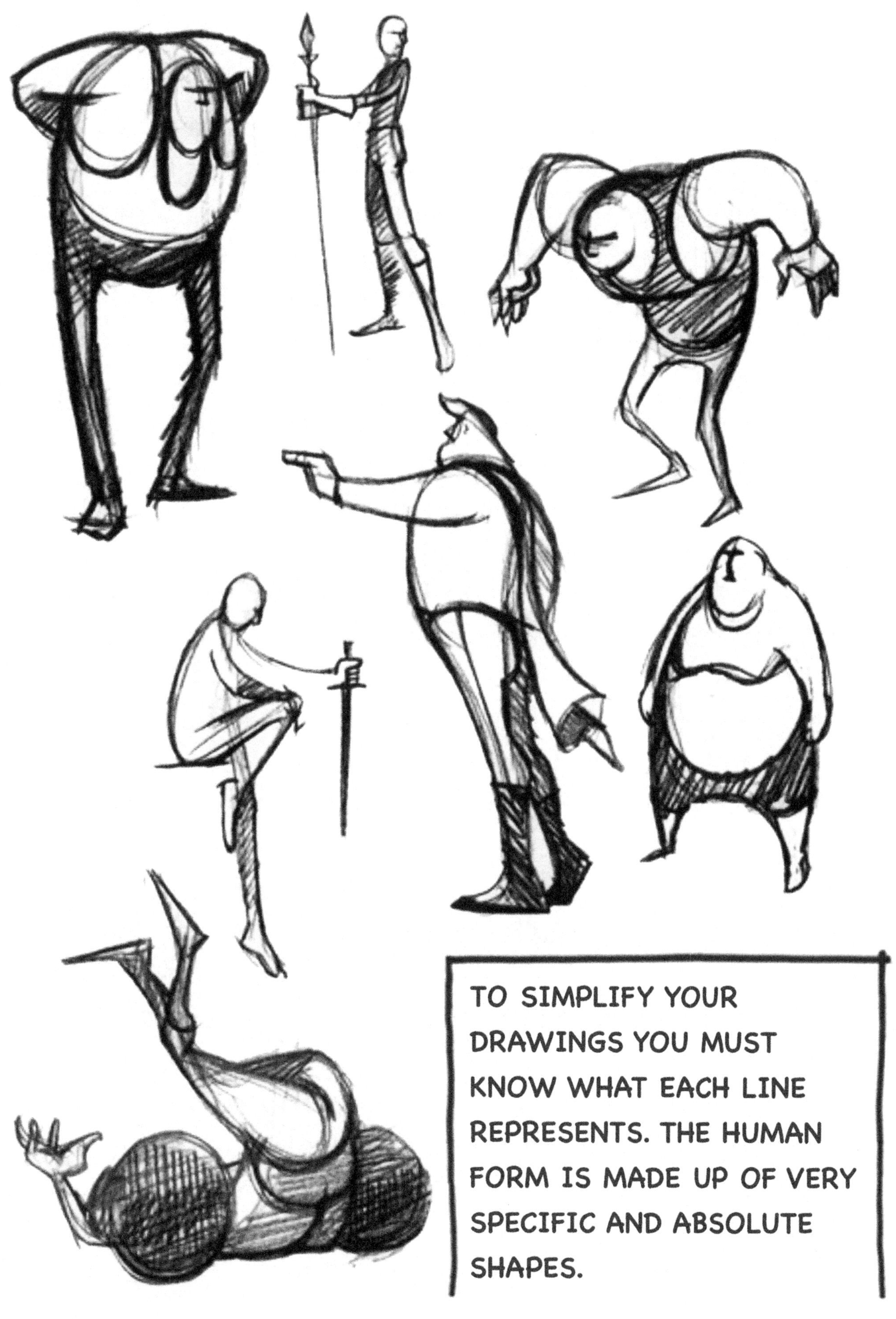

TO SIMPLIFY YOUR DRAWINGS YOU MUST KNOW WHAT EACH LINE REPRESENTS. THE HUMAN FORM IS MADE UP OF VERY SPECIFIC AND ABSOLUTE SHAPES.

In 1935, at the Walt Disney Studio, a series of artist professional development sessions were lead by Don Graham. It has been said that he was responsible for advancing the art of animation more than any other person of the time. The most important session recorded was 'Animating FORCE vs Animating FORM. The session was prompted by the work of Bill Tytla.

It is the understanding of FORCE that will allow you to imply movement and weight with your drawings. In sequential images your animation can imply FORCE which dictates movement, path of action arcs, squash, stretch and delayed action, drag and follow through. It is FORCE that creates the principles of animation.

Two types of FORCE to study are action and acting or motion and emotion. This book focuses on learning how to draw the human form in a simplified manner. This knowledge allows you to represent force in action and emotion through posture when planning animation, illustrations and character designs.

In planning your animation, concentrate on content, the reason for the movement or pose. A simple, clean line, made from knowledge of the subject's form is all that you need. Strive to represent the inner essence of the pose with as few lines as possible, there is little need for detail.

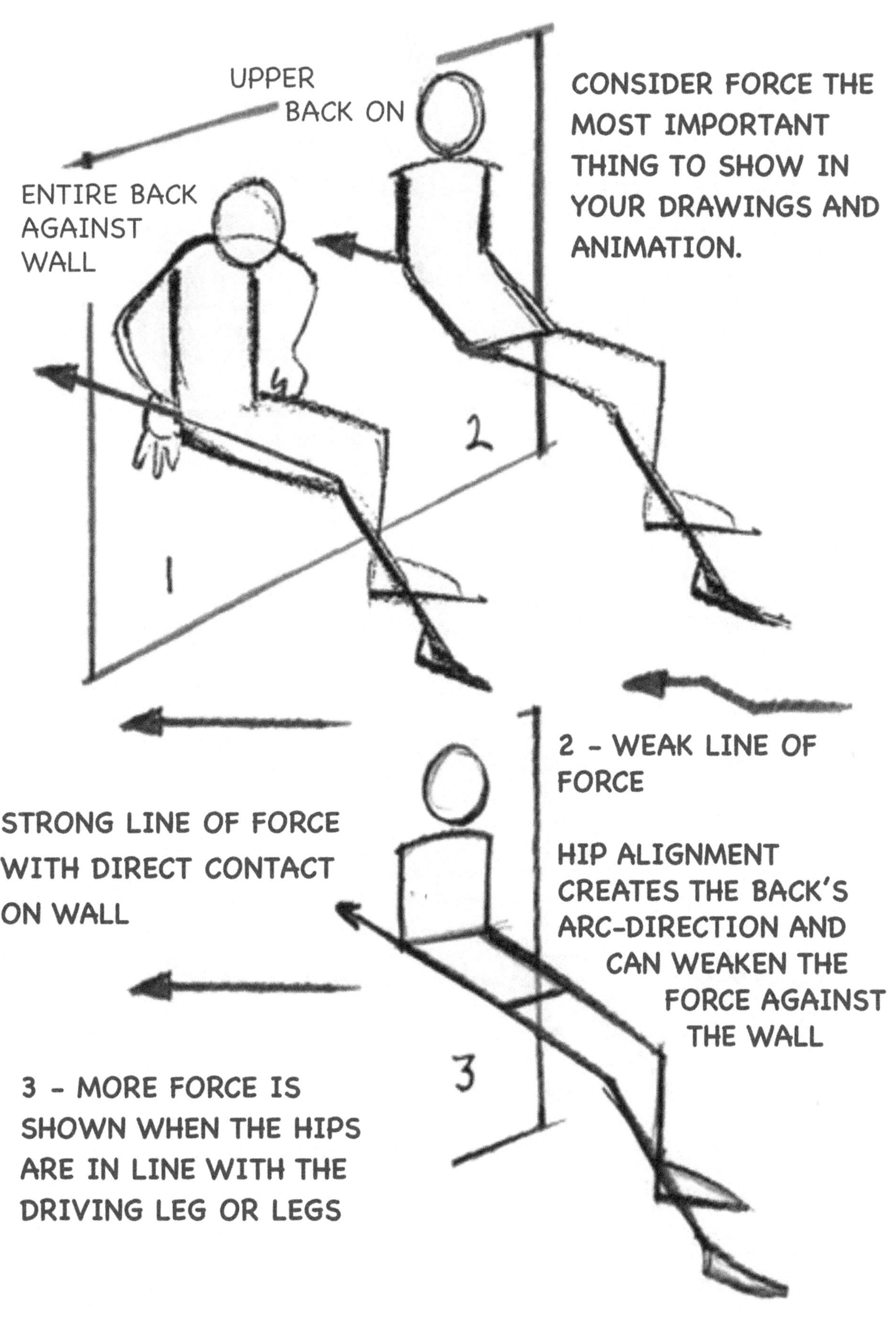

UPPER BACK ON
ENTIRE BACK AGAINST WALL
CONSIDER FORCE THE MOST IMPORTANT THING TO SHOW IN YOUR DRAWINGS AND ANIMATION.
1
2
STRONG LINE OF FORCE WITH DIRECT CONTACT ON WALL
2 - WEAK LINE OF FORCE
HIP ALIGNMENT CREATES THE BACK'S ARC-DIRECTION AND CAN WEAKEN THE FORCE AGAINST THE WALL
3
3 - MORE FORCE IS SHOWN WHEN THE HIPS ARE IN LINE WITH THE DRIVING LEG OR LEGS

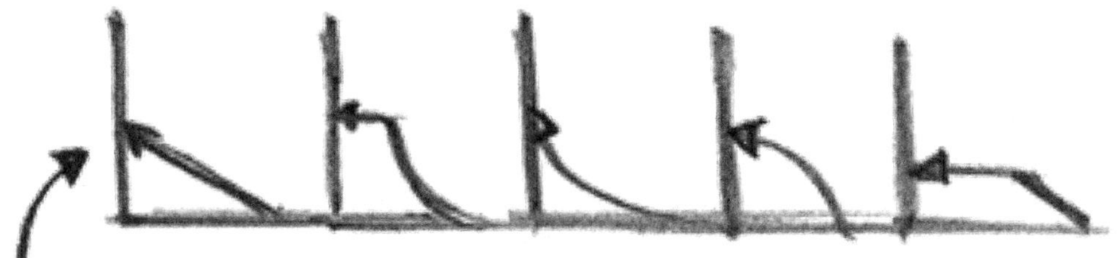

DRAW ONLY LINES AND ARROWS THAT DESCRIBE THE FORCE THAT YOU WANT IN THE POSE, THEN POSE THE CHARACTER INTO THE LINES.

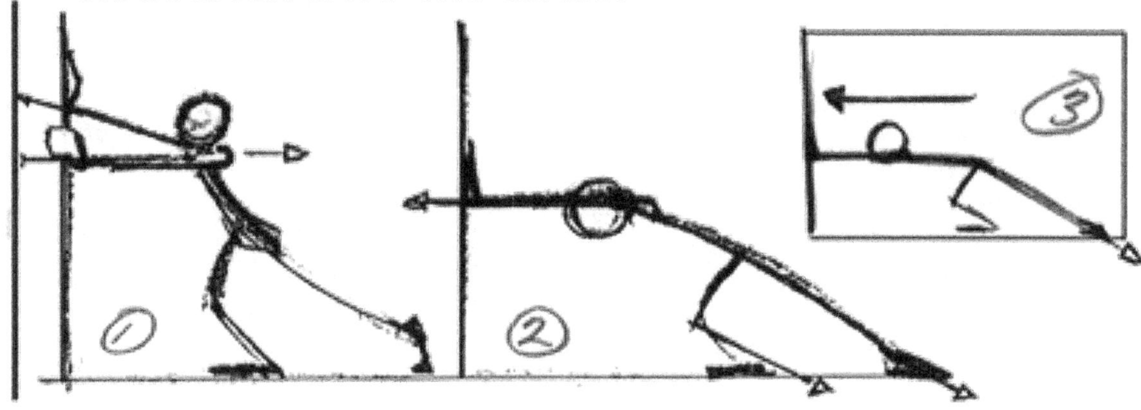

1 - CONCAVE CURVE TO THE BACK SHOWS WEAKNESS OR THE OBJECT IS LIGHT.

2 - MORE DIRECT LINE SHOWS POWER.

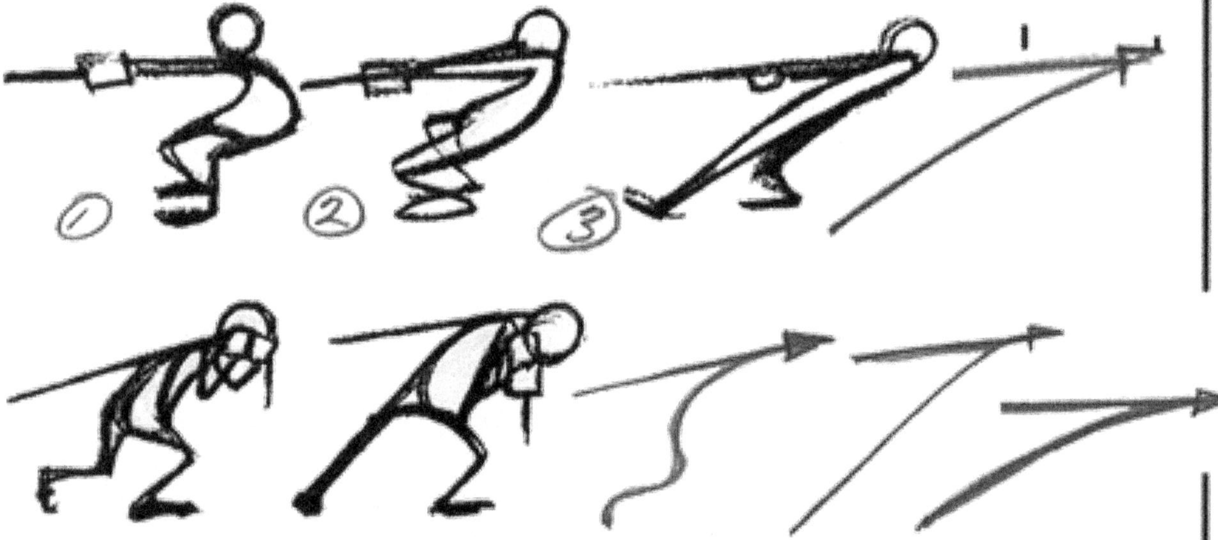

DRAW A SERIES OF ACTION POSES AND START WITH ONLY ARROWS SHOWING FORCE - PUSH, PULL, JUMP, PUNCH... YOUR ANIMATION CAN BE PLANNED WITH THESE SIMPLE LINES OF FORCE.

OPPOSING FORCES

EXERCISE: DRAW A FEW PAGES OF SKETCHES - NO DETAIL, JUST THE IMPORTANT LINE-WORK THAT CAPTURES THE IDEA BEHIND THE DRAWING. SHOW FORCE IN THE POSES.

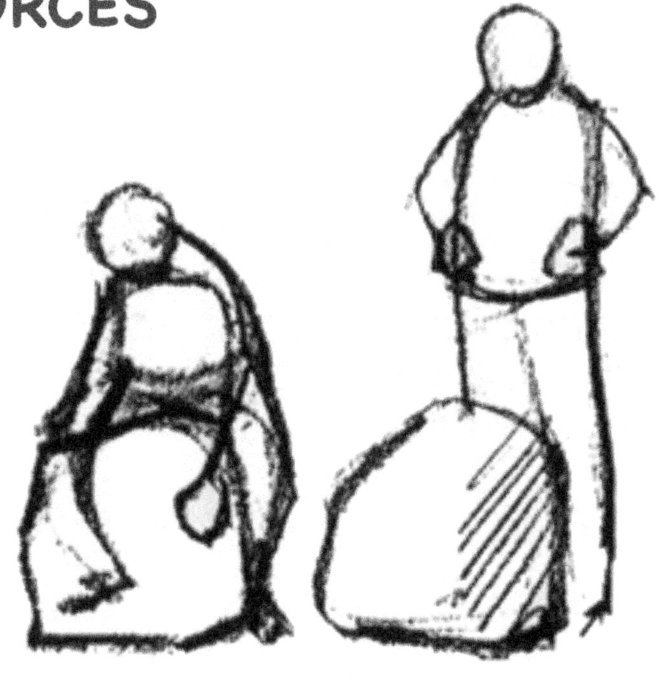

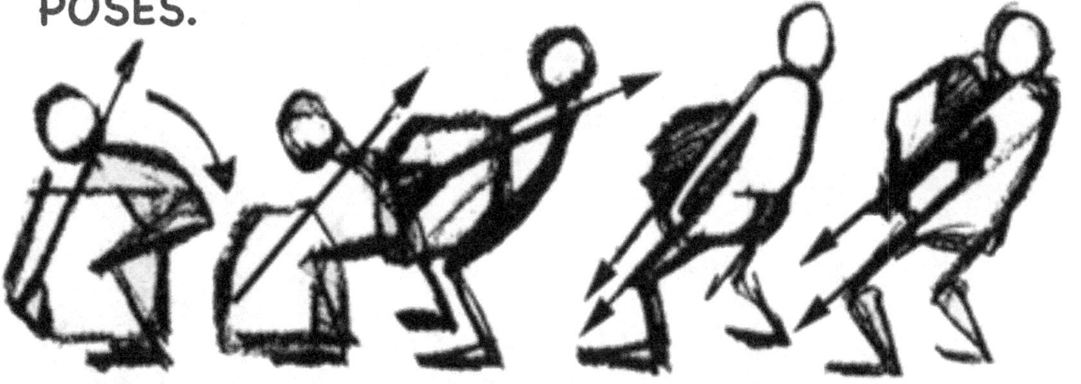

THE NEXT SECTION ON SIMPLIFIED HUMAN ANATOMY WILL MAKE THIS EXERCISE EASIER. WE'RE GOING BACKWARDS REMEMBER

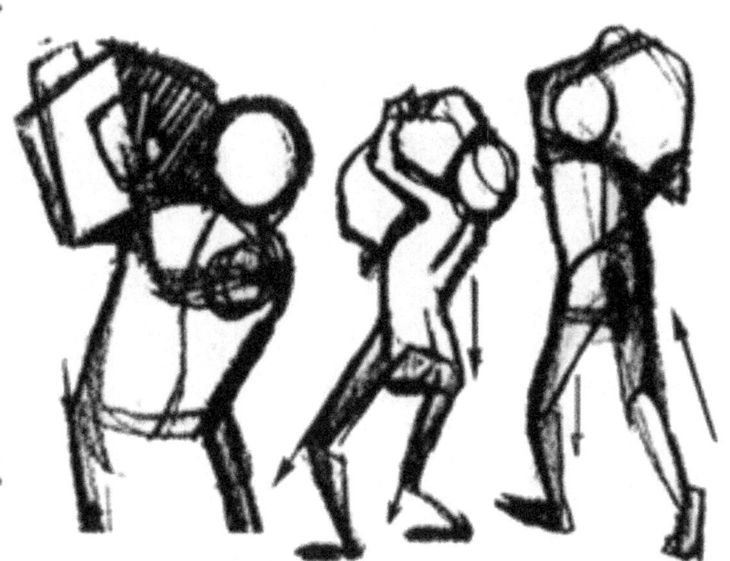

DRAW YOUR CHARACTERS PUSHING, PULLING, LIFTING, CLIMBING OR JUST PICK A SPORT AND START DRAWING. RESEARCH BEFORE YOU DRAW.

OPPOSING FORCES

WHEN THE BODY IS DRIVEN DOWN BY WEIGHT OR FORCE, THE LEGS ACT AS SPRINGS TO ABSORB THE SHOCK - STRIVE TO SHOW THIS IN YOUR DRAWINGS AND ANIMATION.

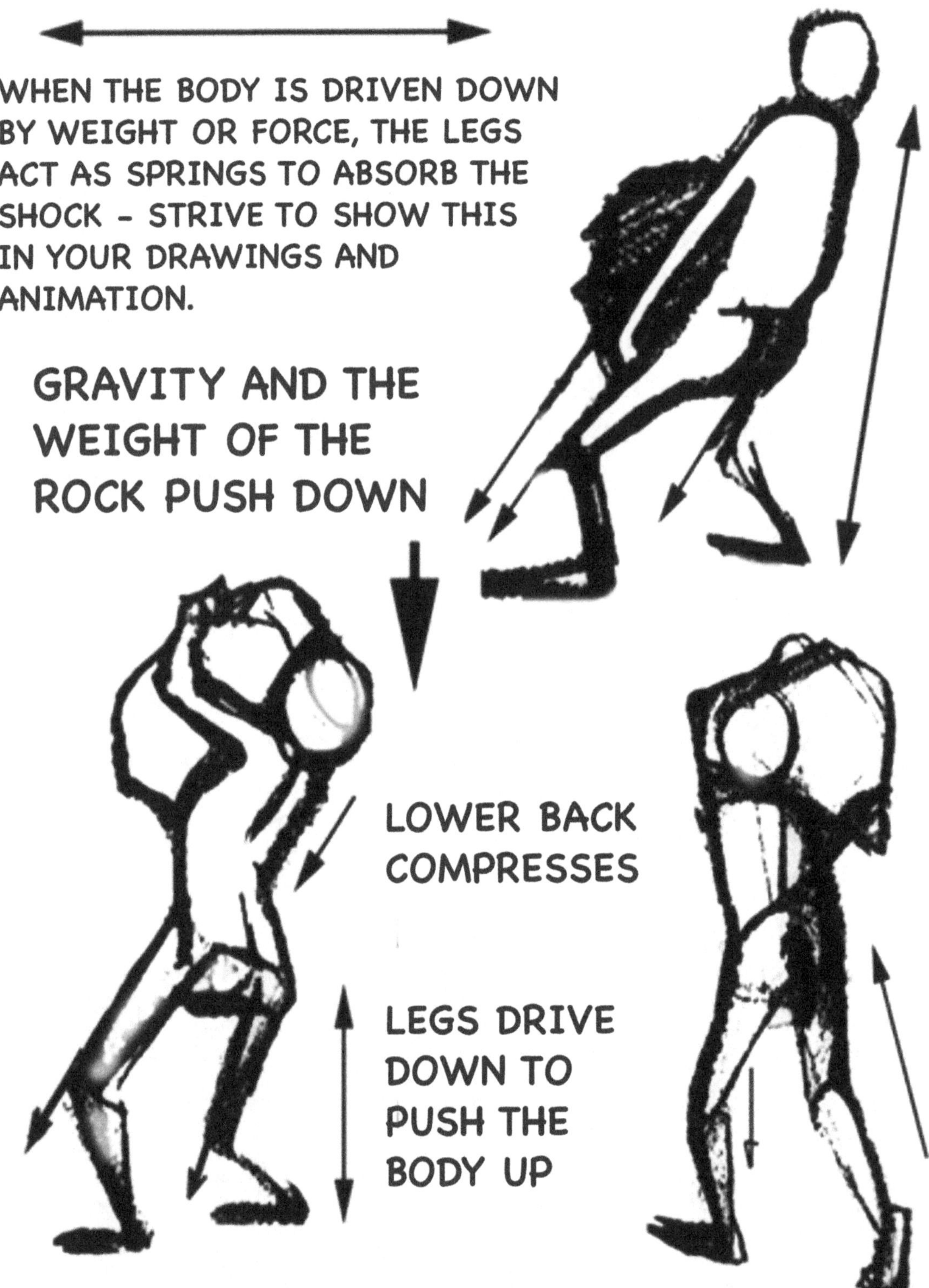

TAKE THE TIME TO UNDERSTAND THE FORCES THAT YOU PLAN TO ANIMATE. DRAW WITH SIMPLE LINE/ARROWS INDICATING FORCE.

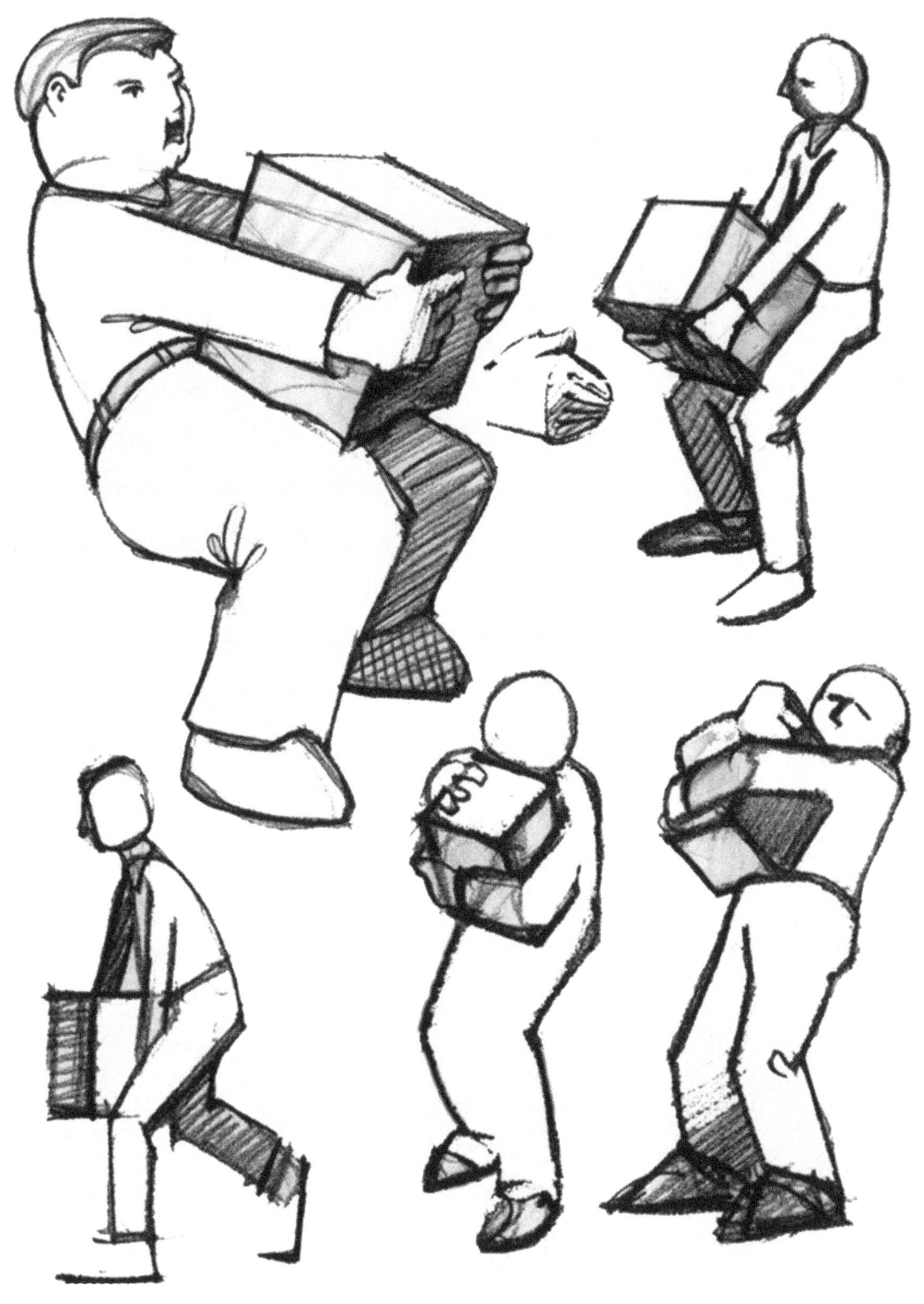

Before you start to animate, be sure that you have found the most entertaining way to tell the story.

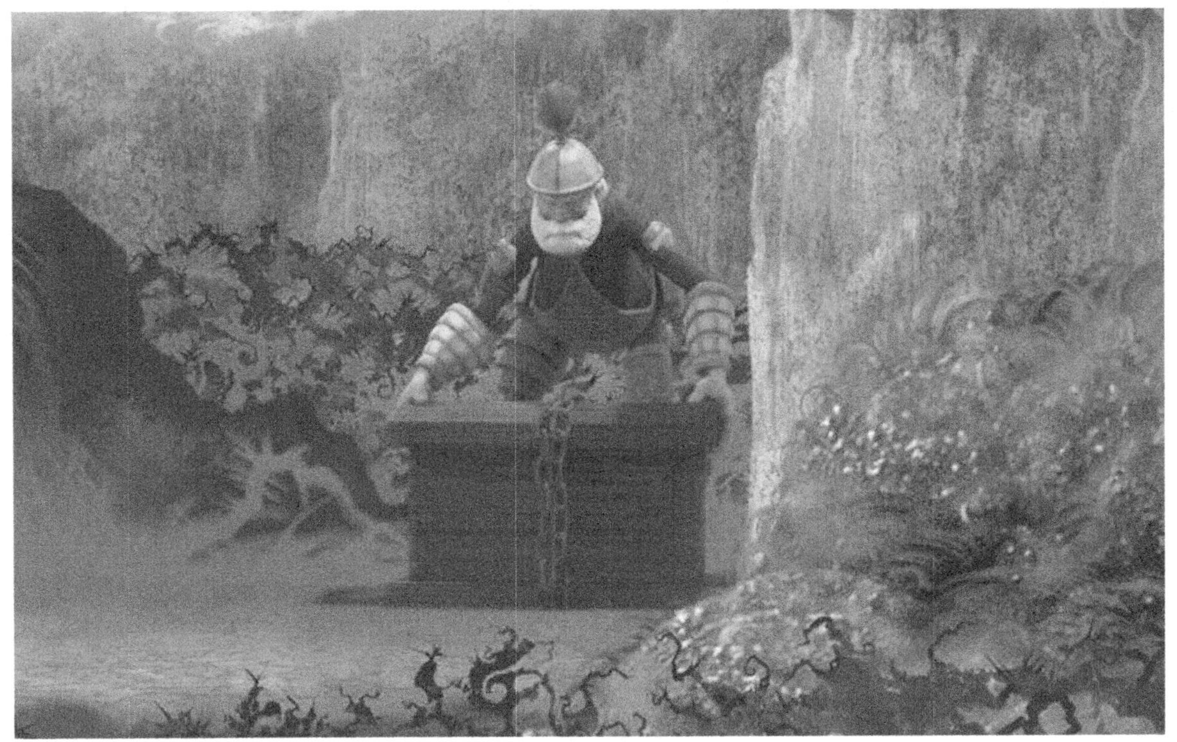

Scenes from an animated short titled LET GO, by the author and many friends at ILM.

Movie files can be seen at www.anamie.com

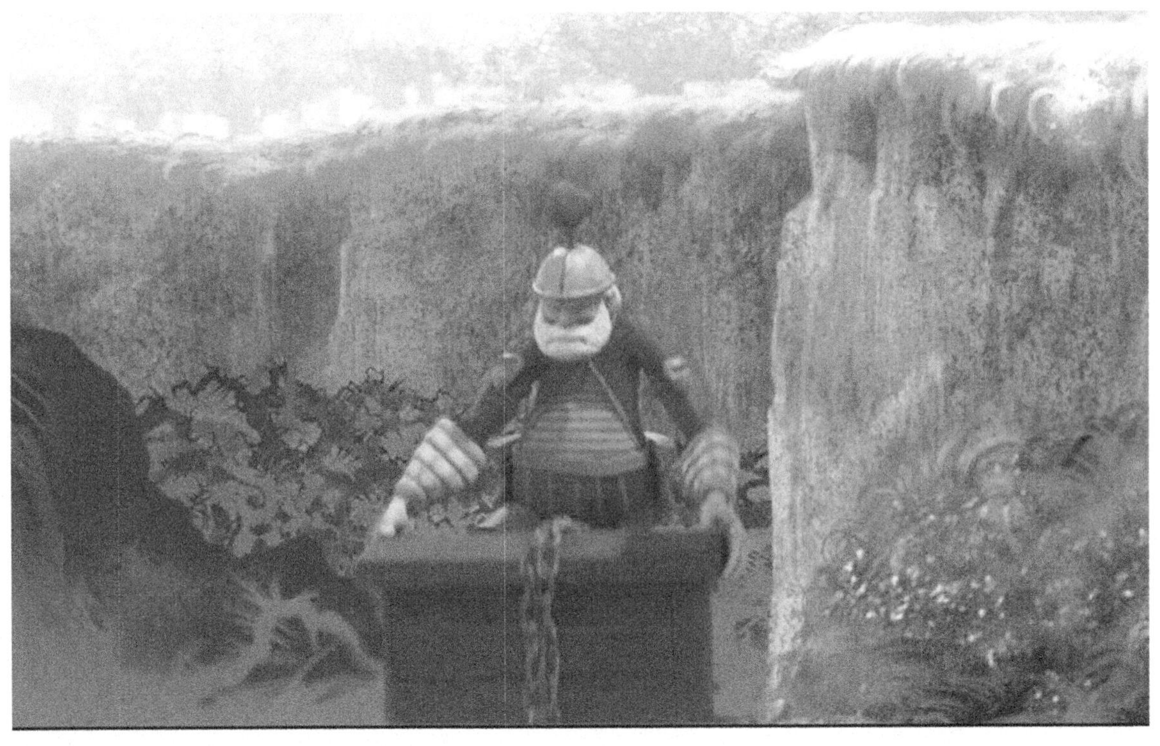

PLANNING ANIMATION

A Senior Lead Animator at ILM said in an interview:
"My best animation is when I have planned thoroughly."
What else need be said?
Planning is fun, it's when inspiration comes to life. Planning is when you get to explore options and make decisions. Without decisions you animate by trial and error. Good animators can tell by looking at someone's planning if key poses or breakdowns are missing or weak, they can even get a sense of intended timing.

Planning should take into account not only the performance and movement of a character but also the aesthetic component of composition in the shot - the "Staging". In the 3D computer animation world you have to make decisions on controller orientation, whether you want IK or FK, if you need constraints or multiple pivot points.

The following pages have exercise suggestions and notes on what to think about when planning animation.

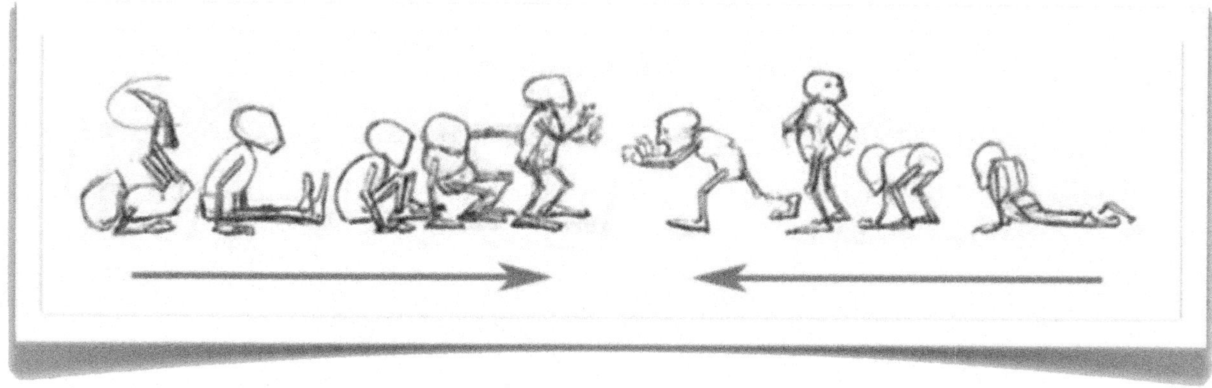

ANIMATION PLANNING

An exercise for the Flour Sac
Weight Shift – Lead and Follow

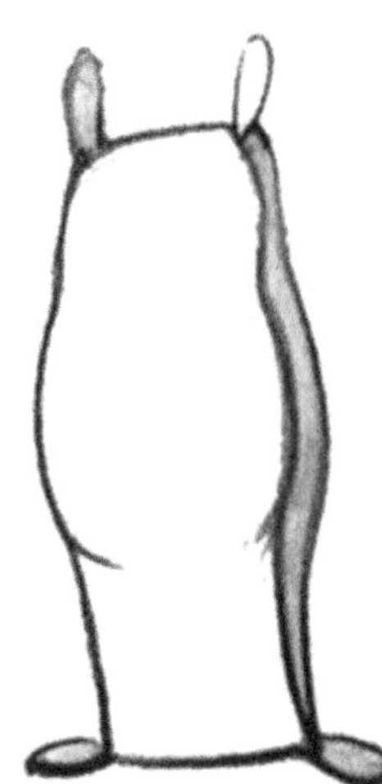

ARC UP

Body mass is
high in the chest

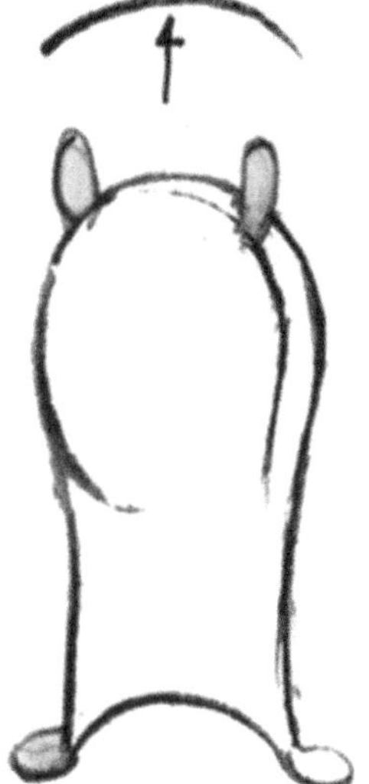

Reverse Arc

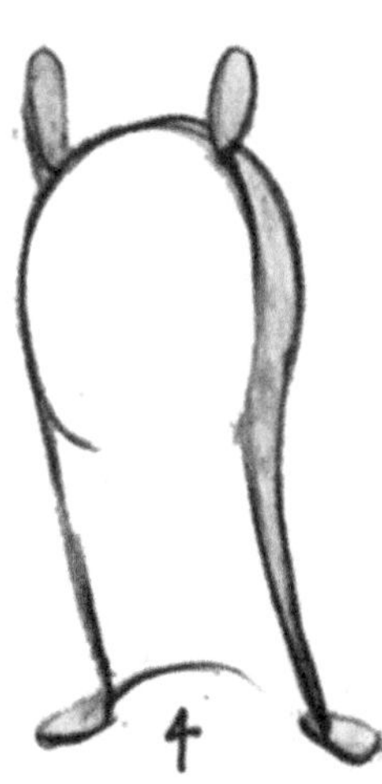

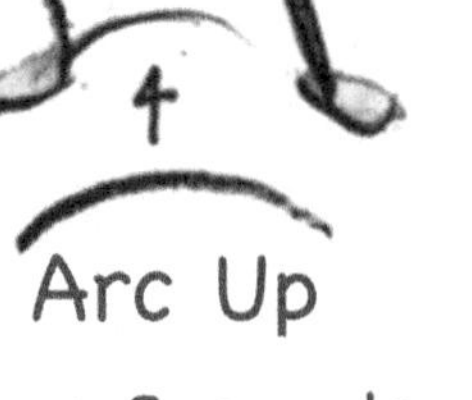

Arc Up

Upper Sac gets
pulled down

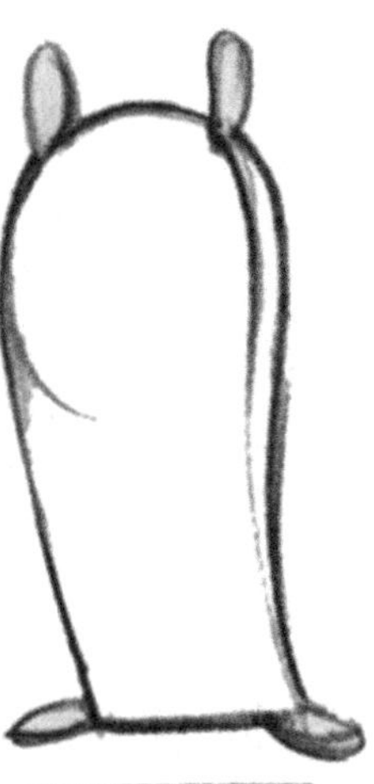

Arc drops
to floor

Body mass
drops and
pulls down
on the top
arc

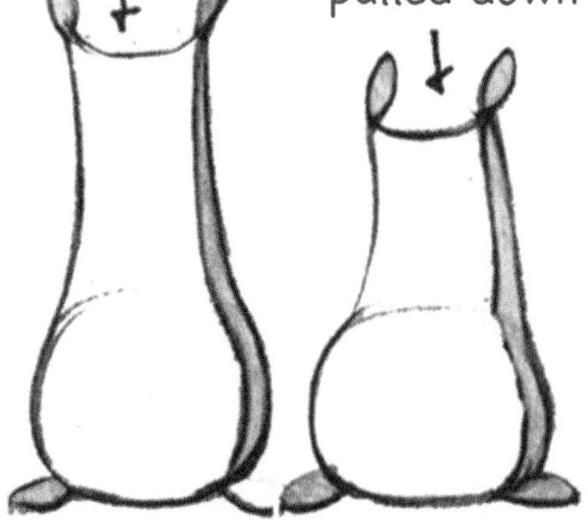

Continue to
compress the
volume down

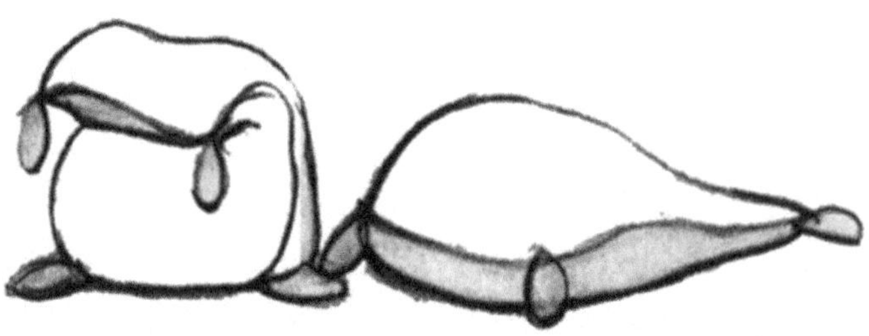

Continue the top down and
roll it back – ears are the
last to drop – timing can
dictate otherwise but that
is the next book

OPPOSING FORCES

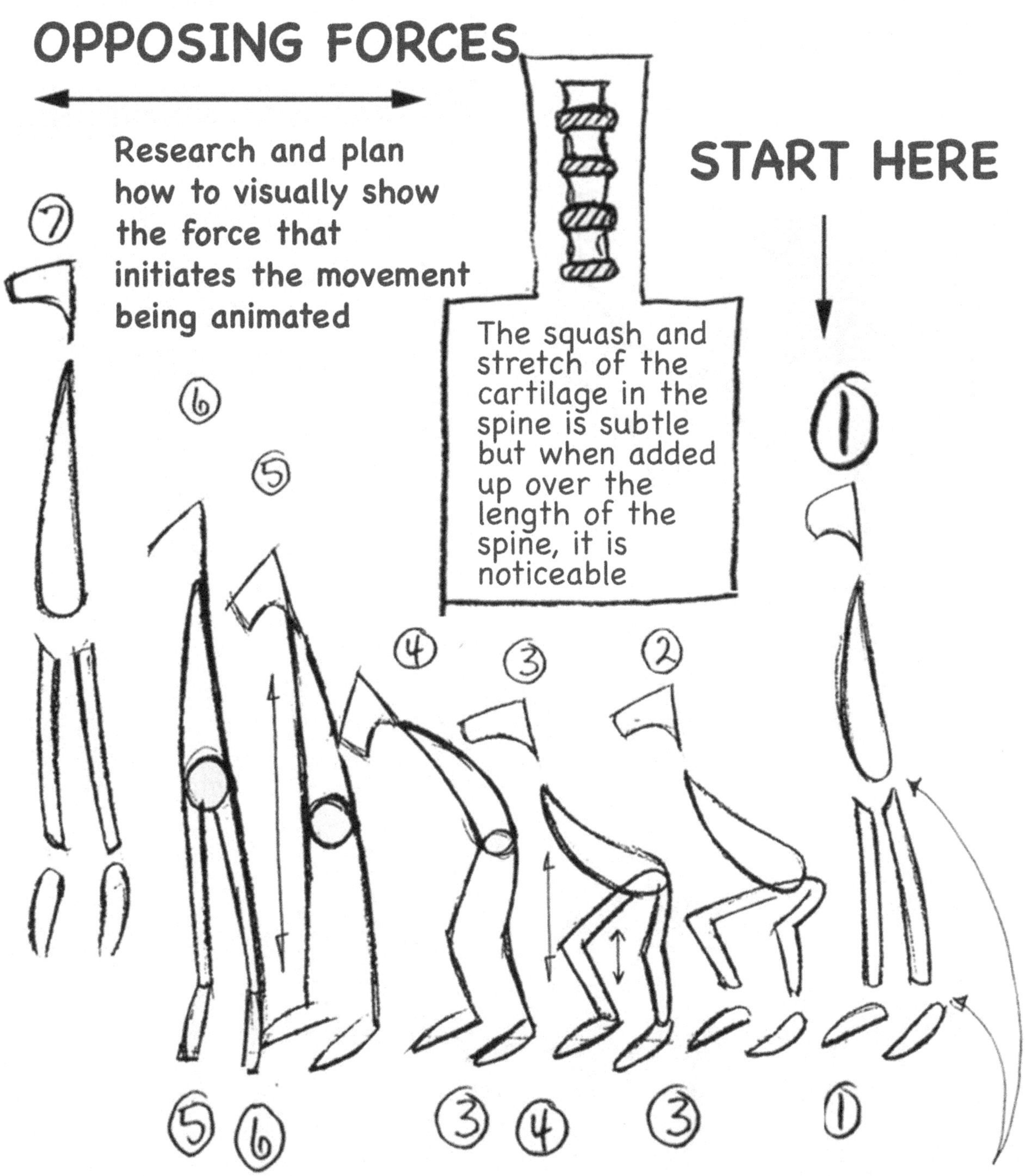

1 - The character is at rest.
2 - Legs bend allowing the body to drop.
  The hips, chest and head follow until at rest in a crouch.
3 - Feet drive down against the ground - the legs drive up.
4 - Lead and follow are created as hips drive up into body,
  arcing back forward, delaying the shoulders and head.
5, 6, 7 - Compression between the main body masses continues
  as long as the body is driven up. Once the feet leave the
  ground, there is no more compression of the body parts
  until landing.

PLANNING TO ANIMATE

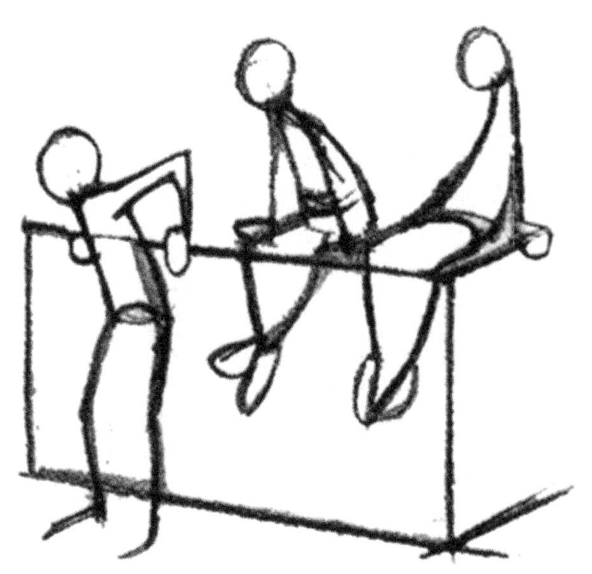

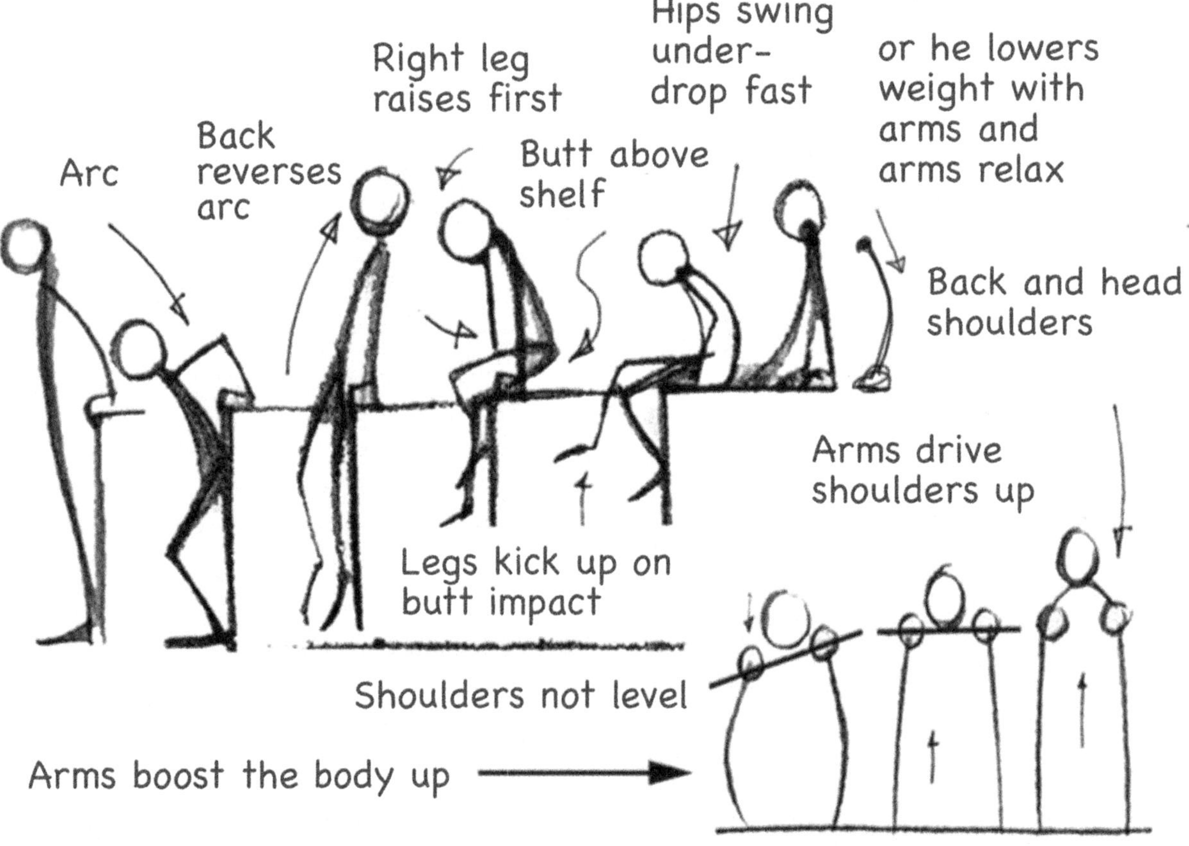

THUMBNAIL YOUR ANIMATION WITH SIMPLE, PRECISE INFORMATION

PLANNING TO ANIMATE

WITH HIS BACK TO THE BOX, HE LOOKS,
TAKES 1 OR 2 STEPS BACK AND SITS DOWN

DO SOME CREATIVE
PLANNING AND MAKE THIS
AN IMPRESSIVE
PORTFOLIO PIECE.

NOT ONLY IS THERE
POTENTIAL FOR BROAD
AND SUBTLE ACTION
ANALYSIS, THERE IS
PLENTY OF OPPORTUNITY
TO BE CREATIVE WITH
THE ACTING.

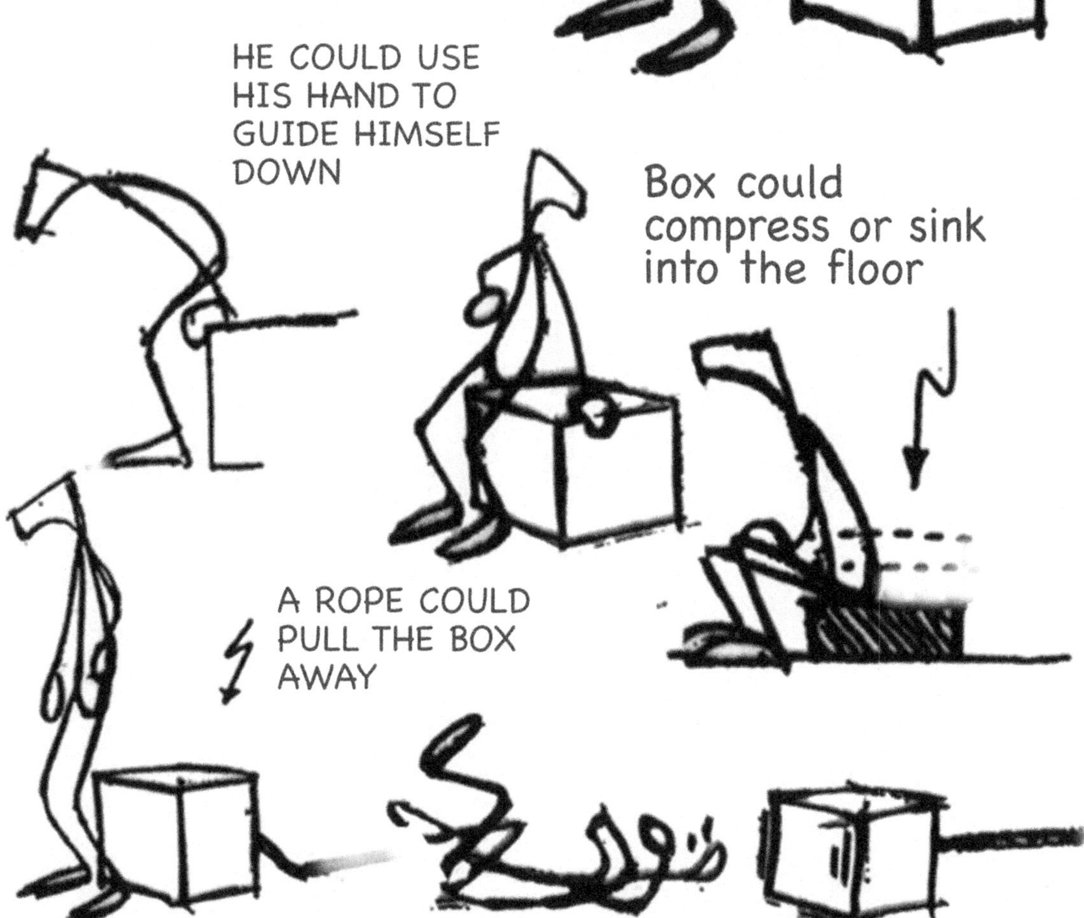

PLANNING WEIGHT SHIFT

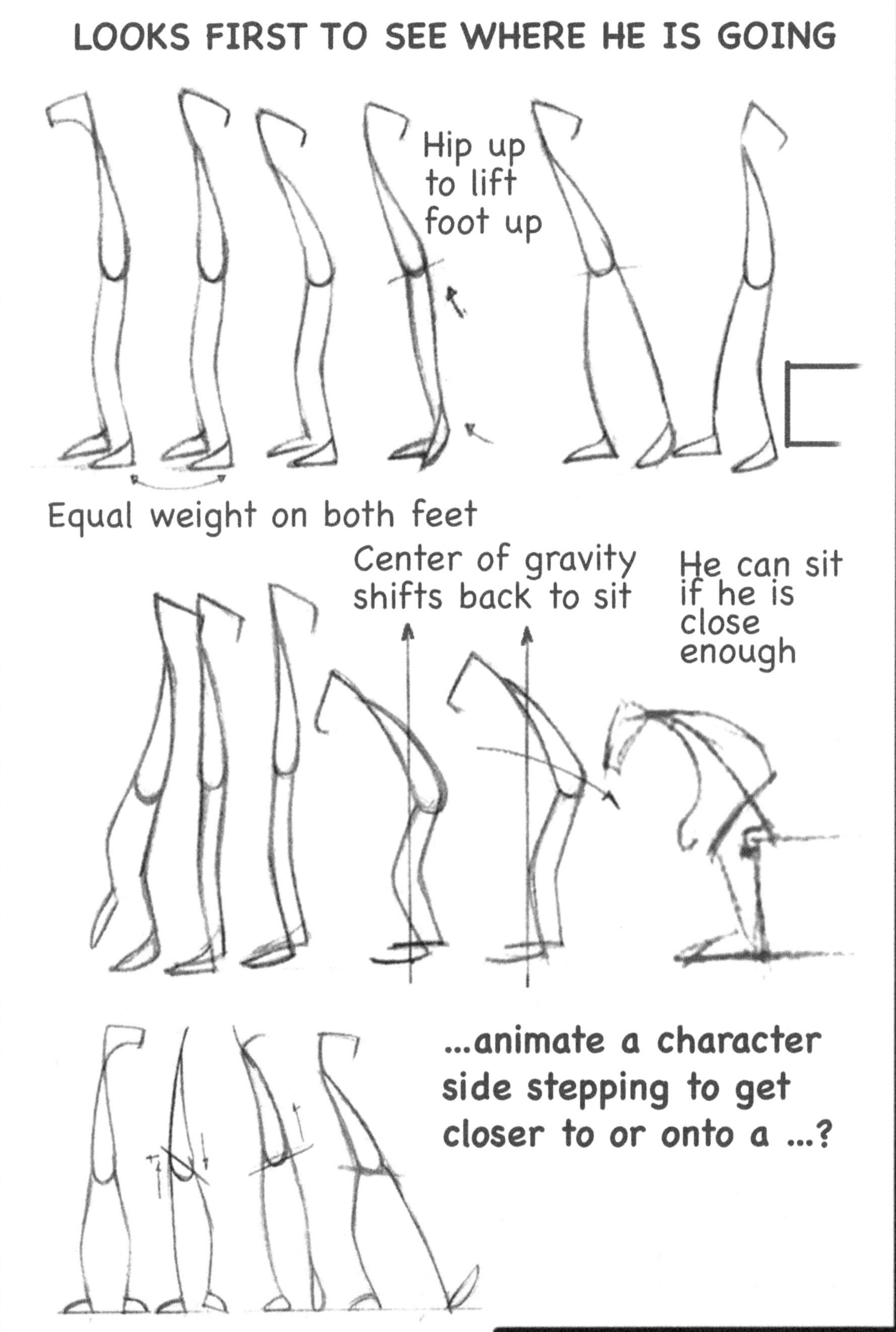

BOX STEP

Here is an example of a seemingly simple exercise. A character steps up onto a box that is approximately knee high.

The next few pages show the planning of the exercise. There are many more options to explore and you will see that not everything researched will be used.

Planning is where creativity comes in to play – the more options you explore the greater the potential for amazing animation. This simple exercise when done well is a very impressive portfolio piece.

All principles of animation must be taken into consideration. What force initiates the movement, weight shift (center of gravity), lead and follow, path of action (arcs), squash and stretch, timing, silhouette ...

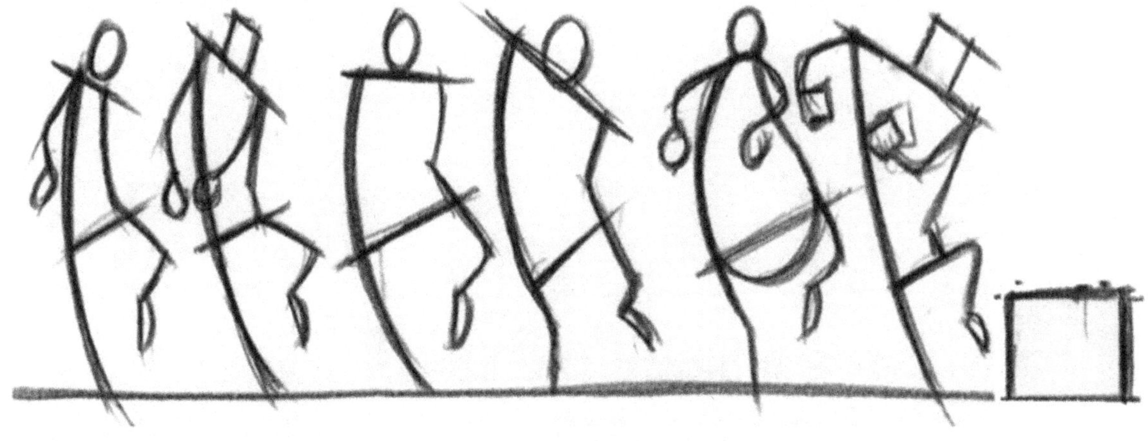

ANIMATION PLANNING

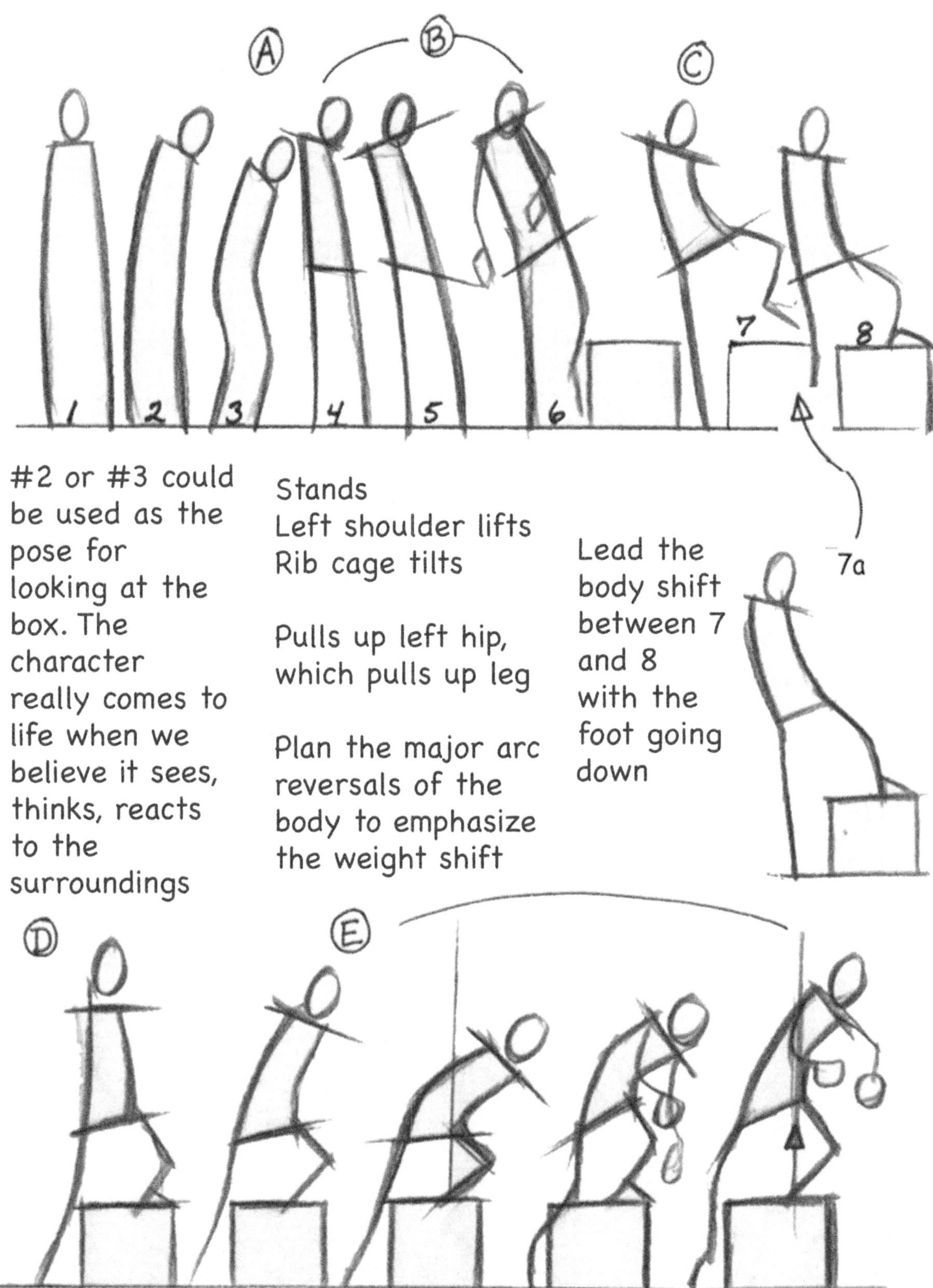

#2 or #3 could be used as the pose for looking at the box. The character really comes to life when we believe it sees, thinks, reacts to the surroundings

Stands
Left shoulder lifts
Rib cage tilts

Pulls up left hip, which pulls up leg

Plan the major arc reversals of the body to emphasize the weight shift

Lead the body shift between 7 and 8 with the foot going down

A-B-C-D-E indicate the body curve or arc reversals, some are more dramatic than others

BOX STEP

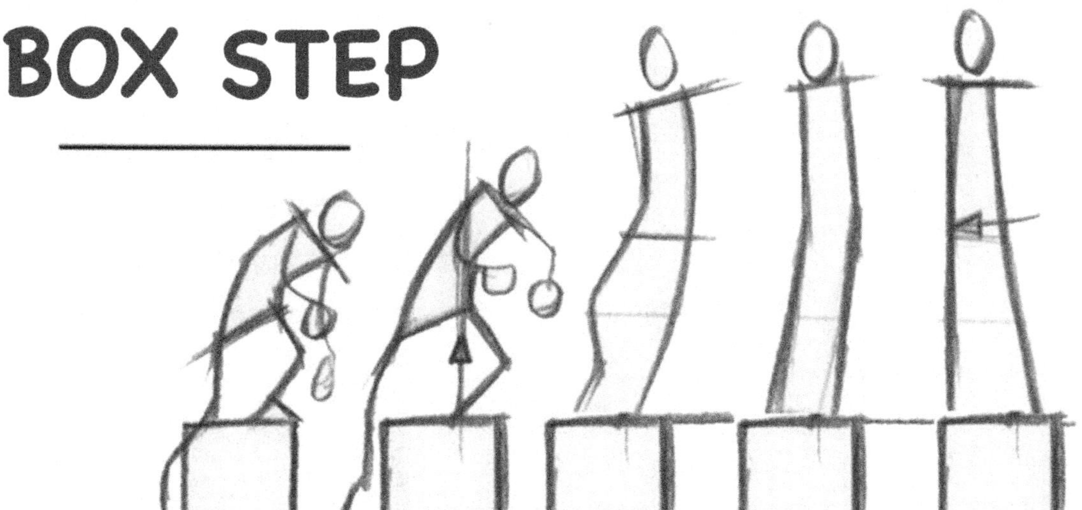

Plan major body movements such as weight shift first. Show arms when they are needed to support the movement or help balance the pose. Do not overlook the planning of the arm movements before you begin to animate. Explore the many options for each part of the action.

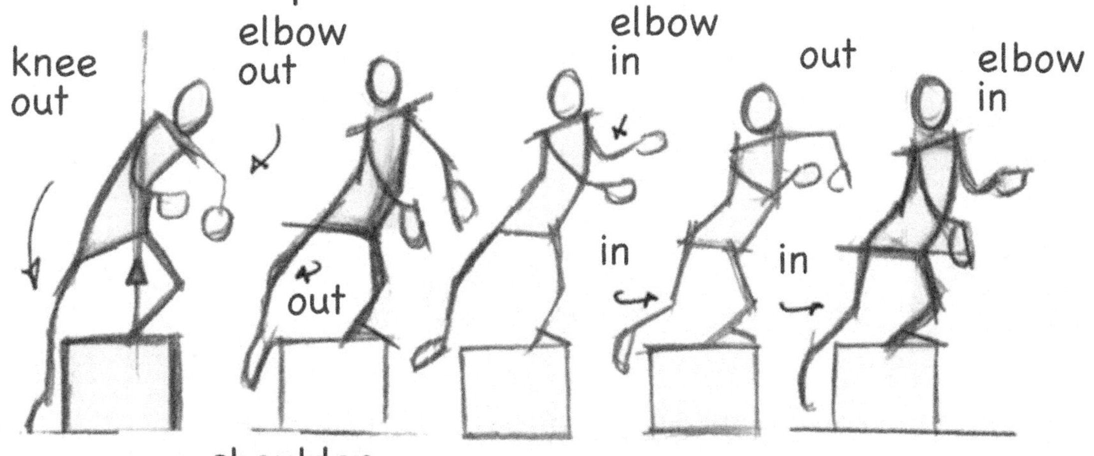

The first example on the next page is using the sketches from the book. A few have been removed for smoother flow.

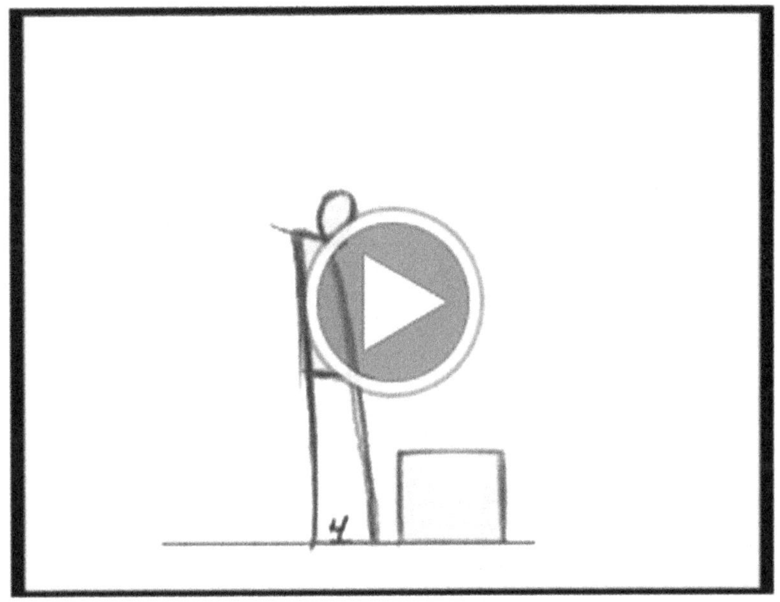

This test was done using the planning drawings from the previous pages.

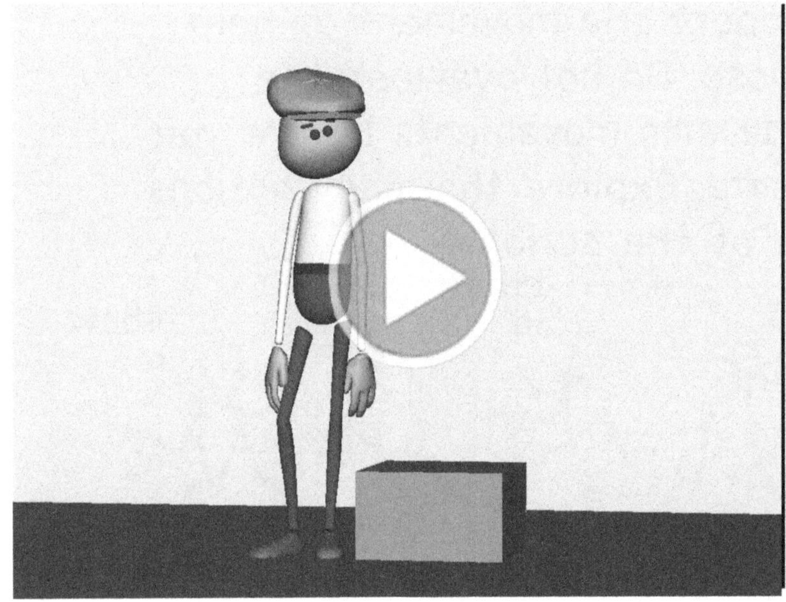

Here are a few examples of a side step.

Movie files can be seen at www.anamie.com

VanArthur, the guy with the hat, is used with permission from Vancouver Institute of Media Studies, Vanarts www.vanarts.com

Stewie, the guy with the big head is used with the permission of Animation Mentor, 'Next Education LLC' www.animationmentor.com

The Pitch

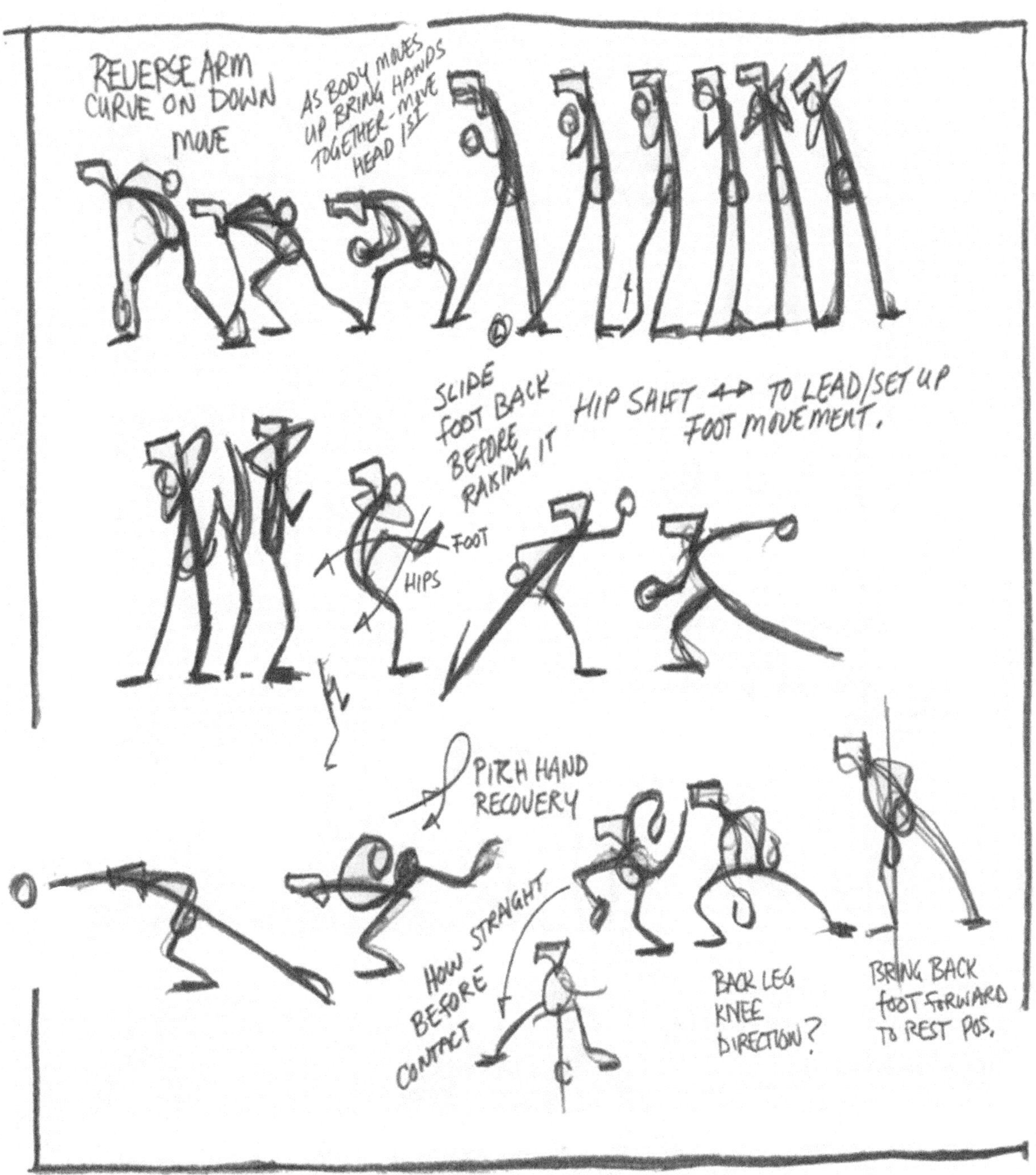

This is an example of a planning page. Sometimes the first pass sketches only make sense to the person planning. Stay loose and informative. You are exploring options from which decisions will come. Don't get hung up on details, use simple structure and proportions. Impress your animation director with information.

SIMPLE THOUGHTS FOR PLANNING HOW TO SHOW WEIGHT

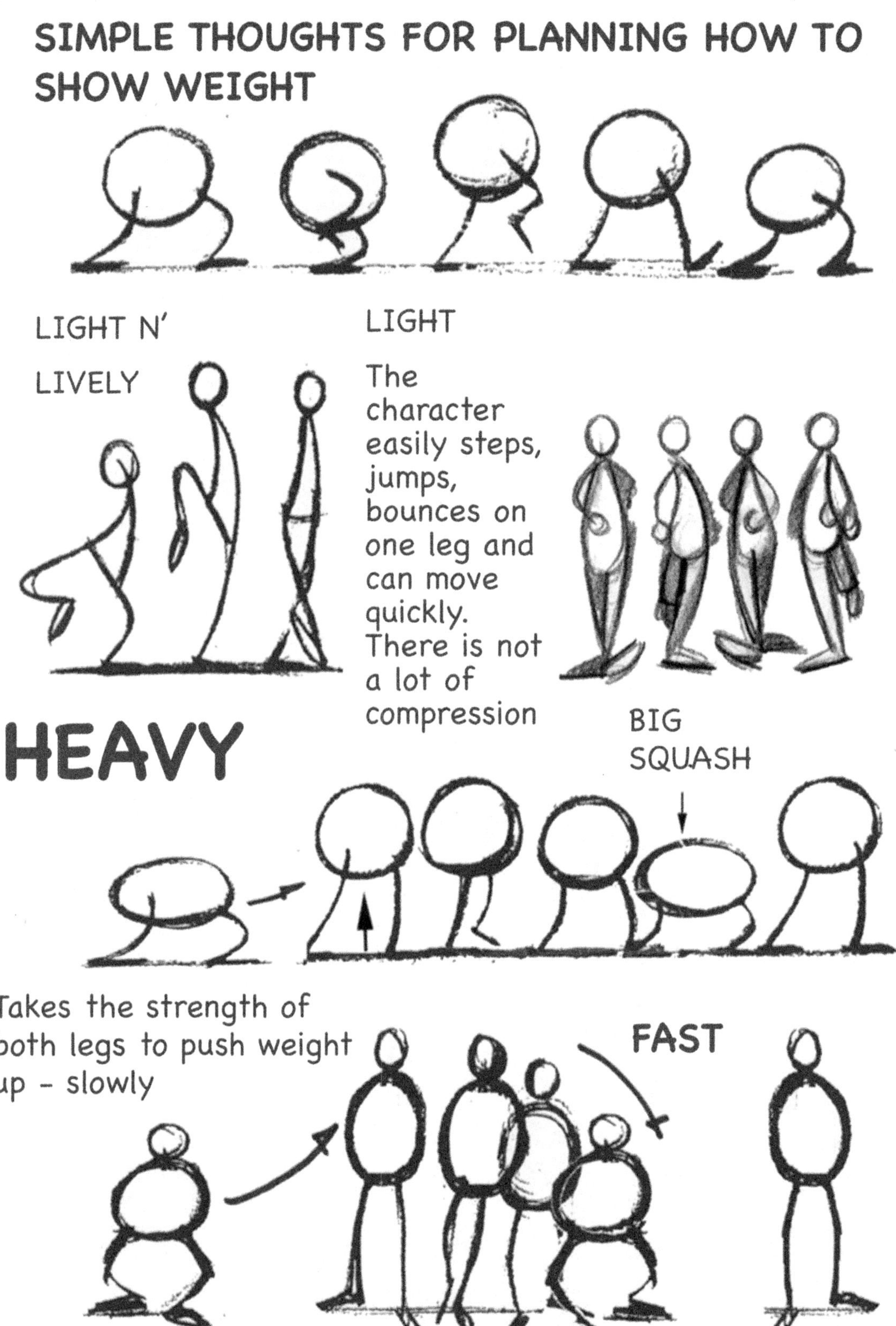

To show heavy - both legs are needed to force the body up slowly. A heavy character spends little time on one leg and there will be plenty of compression (squash) when the character goes down. It takes the strength of both legs to slow the body down during compression.

HEAVY SUITCASE PULL

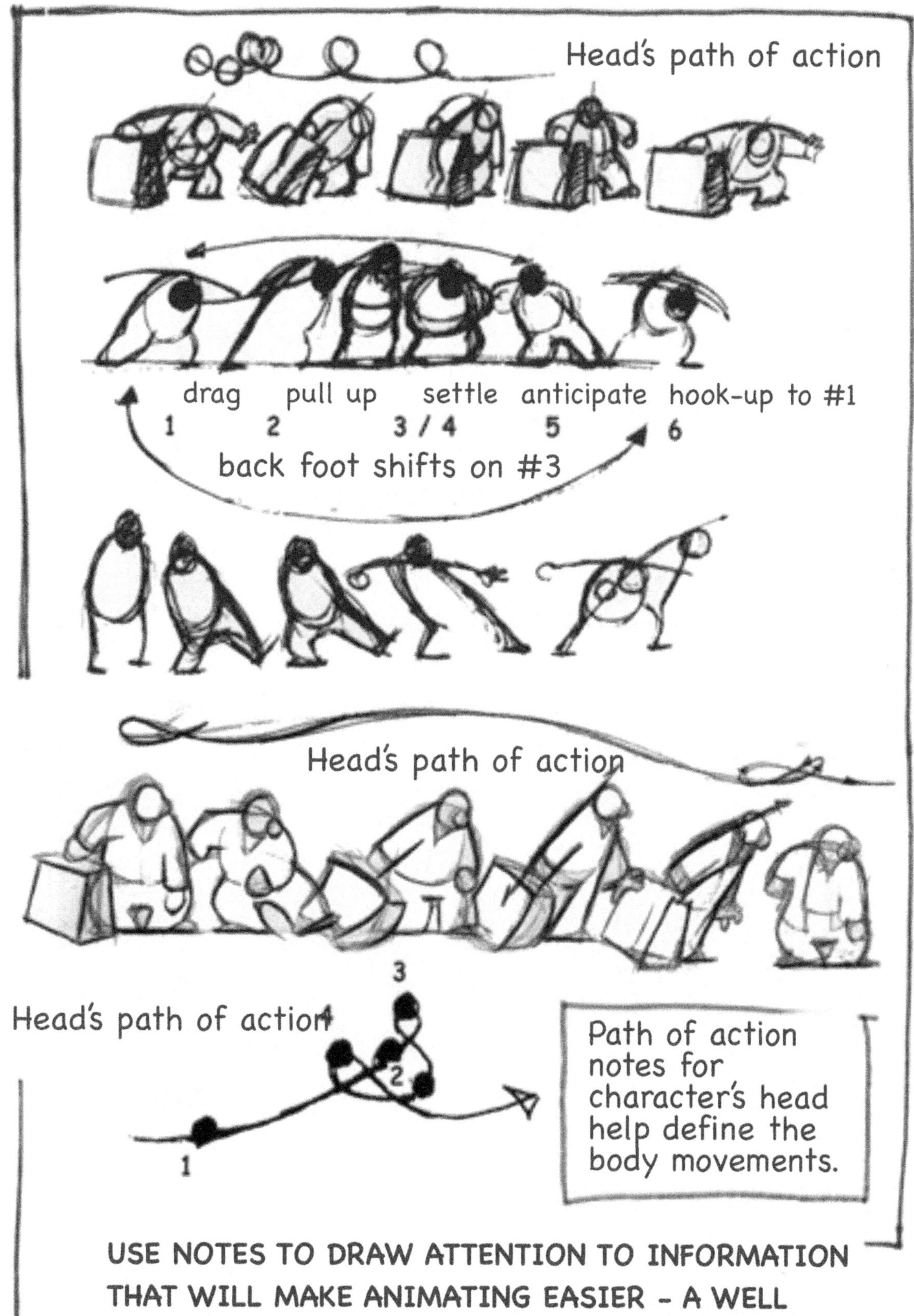

USE NOTES TO DRAW ATTENTION TO INFORMATION
THAT WILL MAKE ANIMATING EASIER - A WELL
PLANNED PATH OF ACTION FOR THE HEAD, HANDS, HIPS,
MAKES COMPLETING THE SHOT FAST, EASY, FUN.

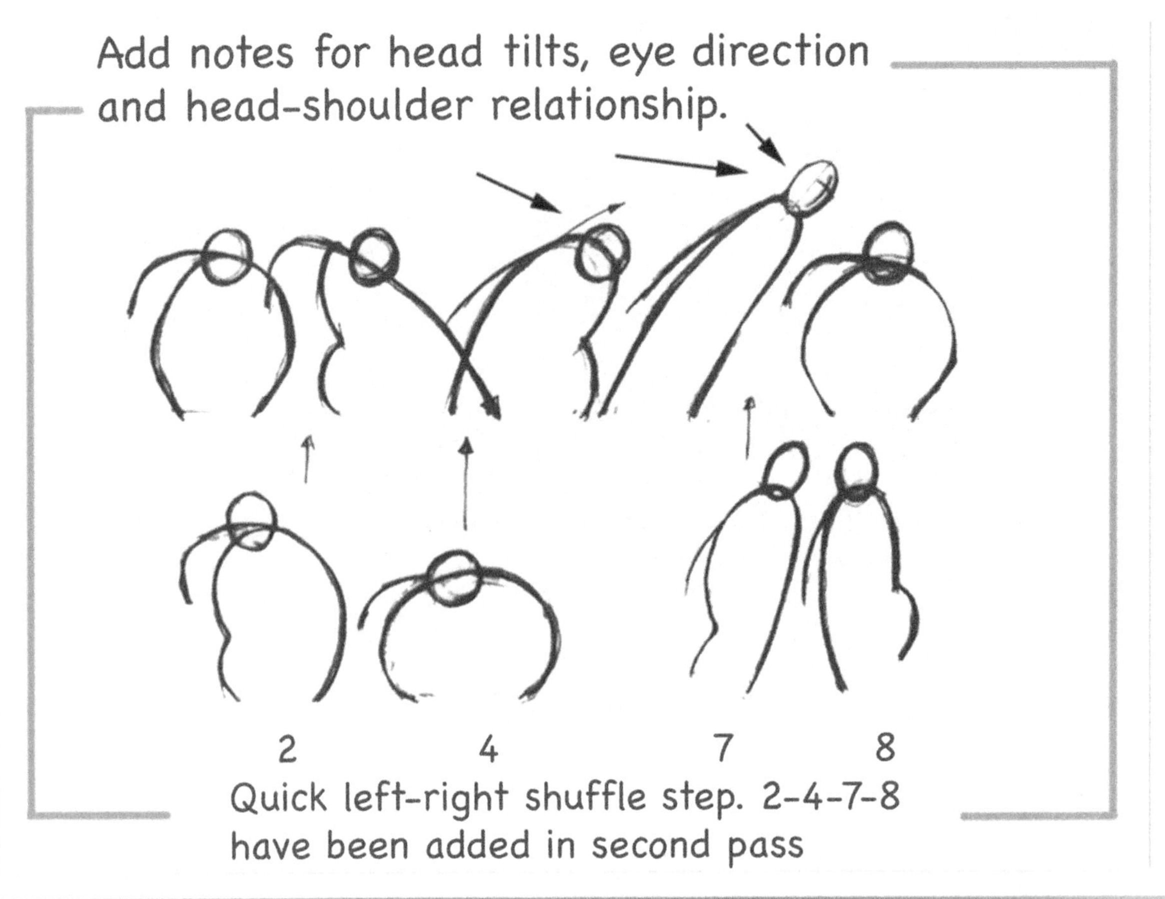

Add notes for head tilts, eye direction and head-shoulder relationship.

Quick left-right shuffle step. 2-4-7-8 have been added in second pass

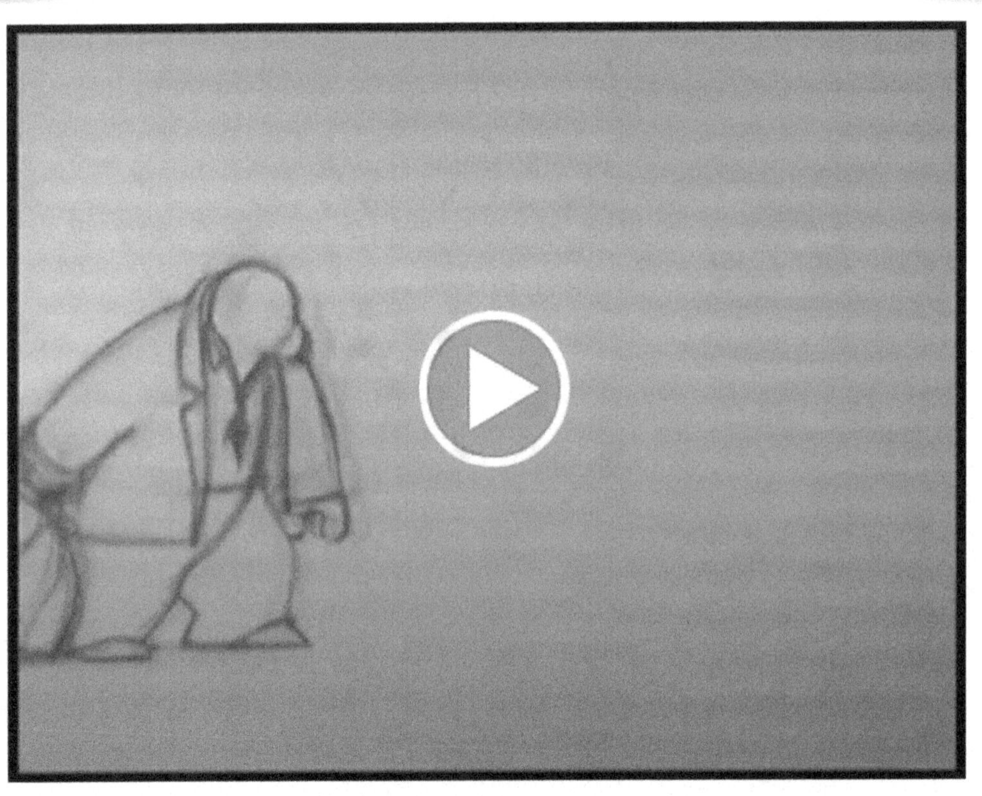

Movie files can be seen at www.anamie.com

BALANCE * WEIGHT * FORCE

This exercise is to plan the animation of a character lifting a very heavy ball onto a ledge

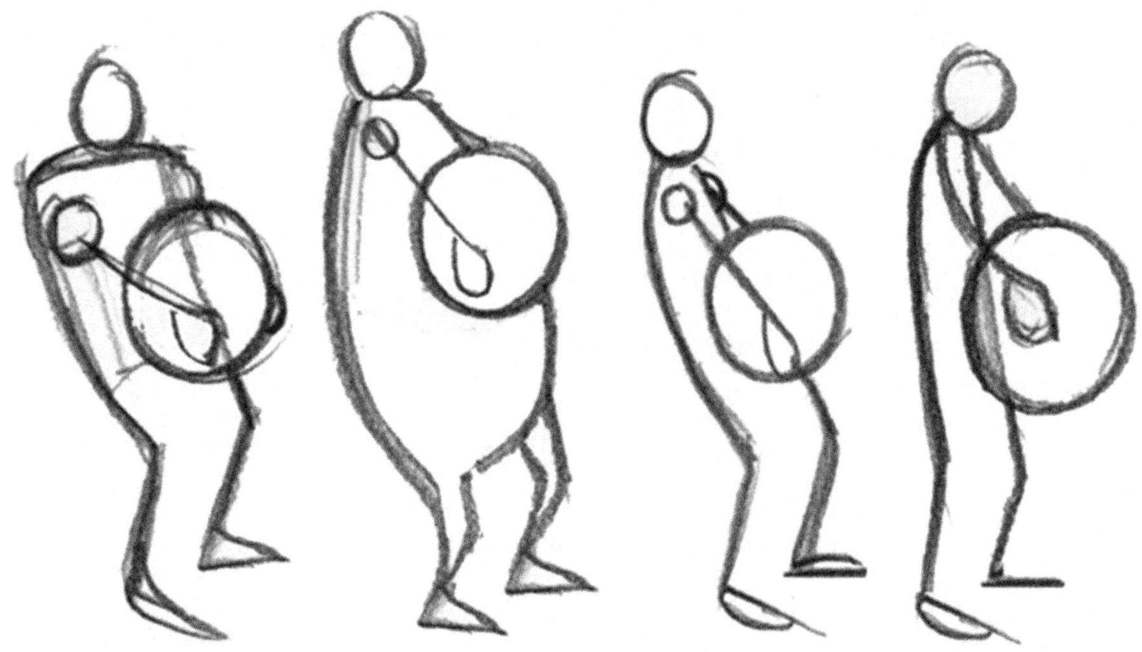

The design of the character is not as important as the content of the drawing. Be precise with the information about balance, weight and force in your sketches before you start animating.

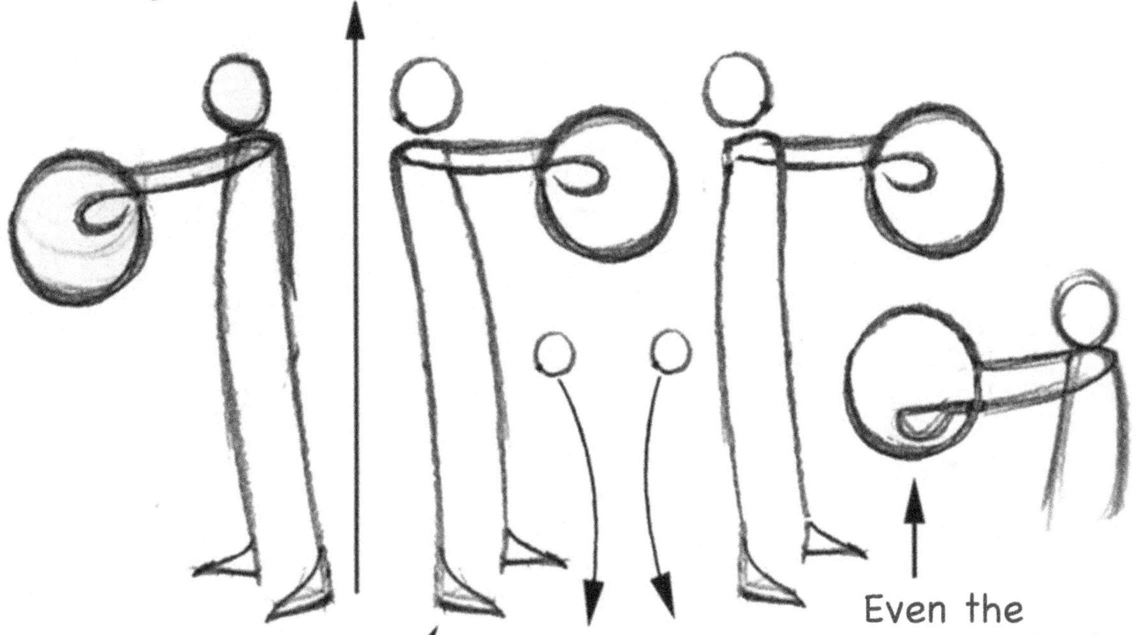

The body leans back to counter balance the weight of the ball.

What body arc best describes what you want to show?

Even the placement of the hands on the ball implies how heavy it is.

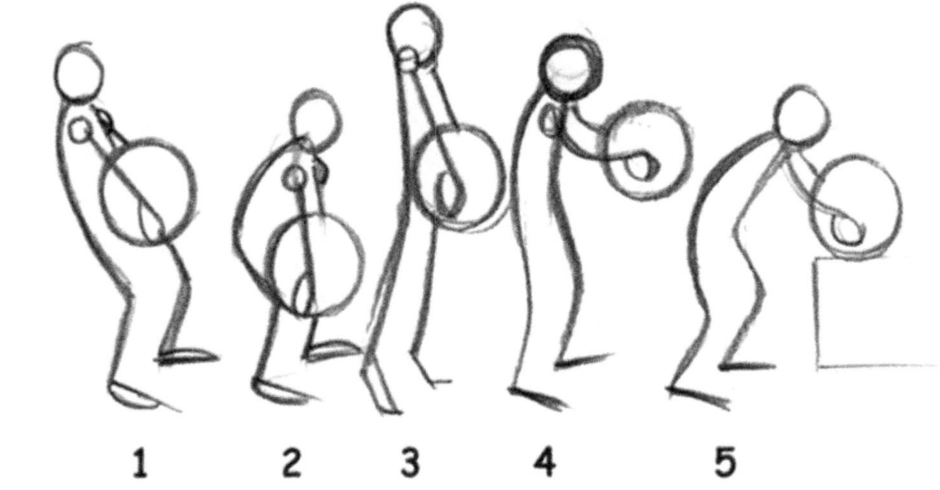

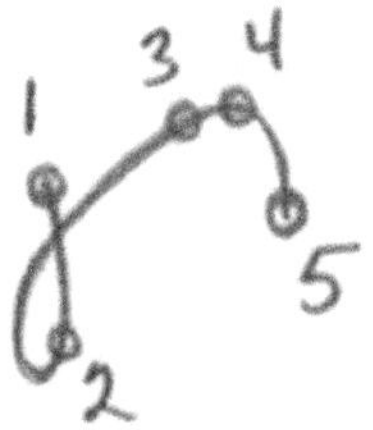

A possible path of action:
1-2 the ball is lowered and without stopping, it arcs back and is driven up by the legs and pulled up by the arms to position 3. The ball slows and arcs to drop almost straight down - 4-5.

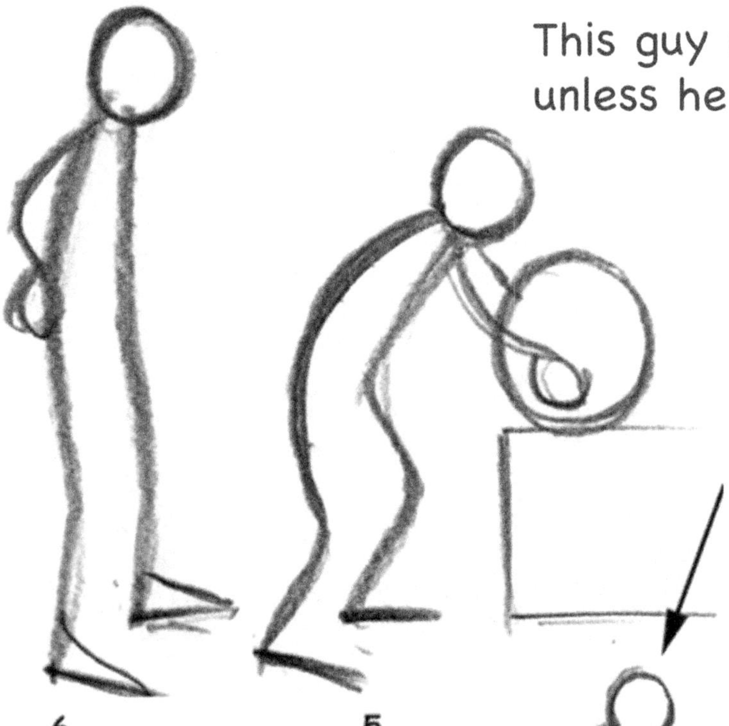

This guy cannot stand up unless he adjusts his balance.

Part of his weight in 5 is supported by his arms. If he moves his hands before shifting his weight he does a face plant.

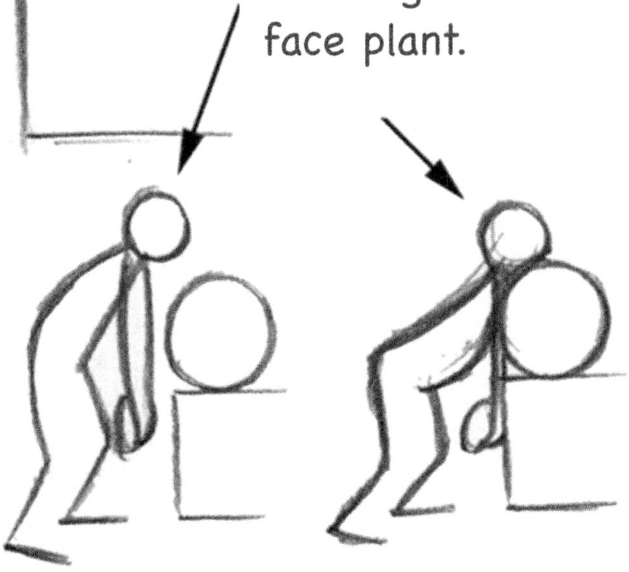

HOW DO YOU GET FROM HERE TO HERE?

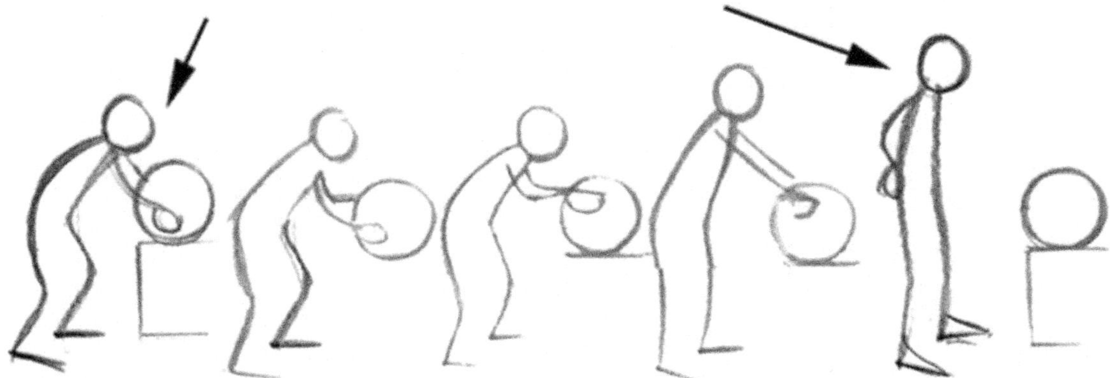

Move one hand up at a time, push back and stand up to a balanced stance

Move one hand to the top of the ball and push back

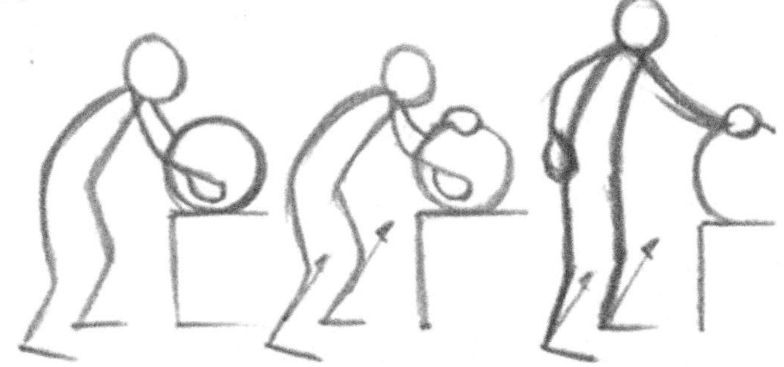

Legs straighten up as he pushes back

Drop hands back to the table, shift hips back and stand up

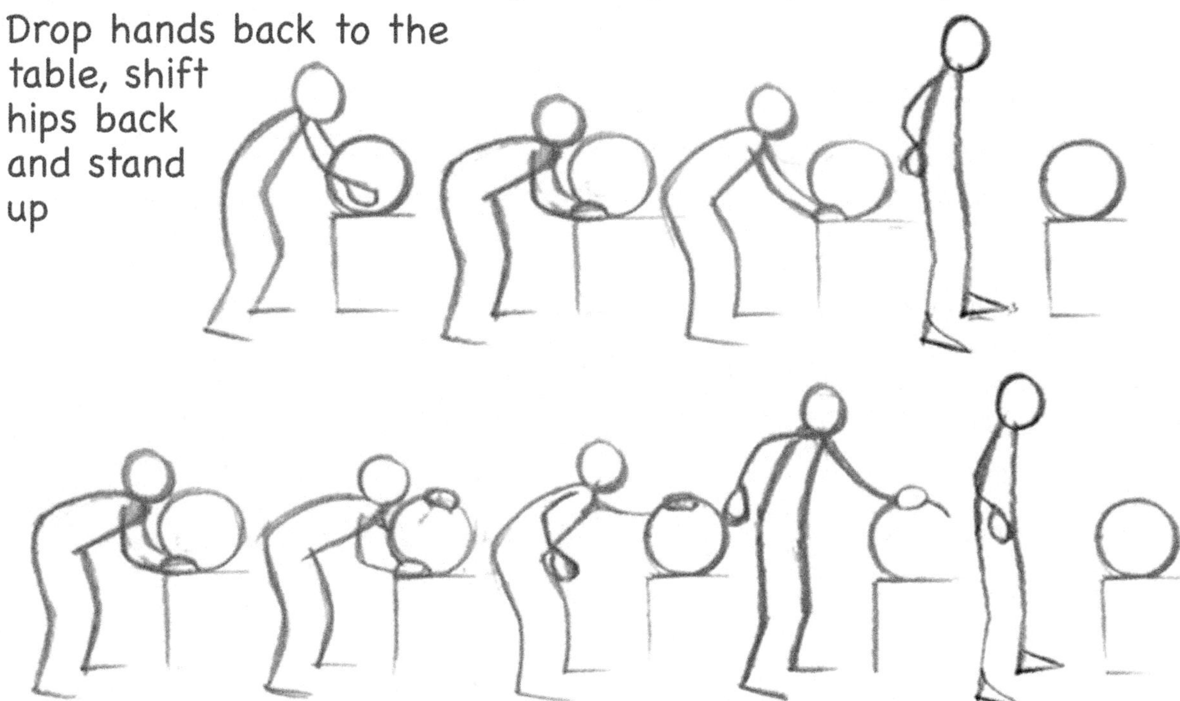

Drop hands to the table, move one to the top of the ball to steady his balance as he pushes to shift his hips back so he can stand up - or - steps closer to the ball so he doesn't have to support weight with is hands.

Planning Animation With Simplified Drawing

Decide what action to animate and define the forces that create that action. Example: a character jumps on to and off a box. Will it just be an action analysis exercise or will there be acting in it? Acting means that you are going to reveal character through timing, posture and movement.

There are many questions to be answered before you start animating.

THE CHARACTER: appearance, strength, emotional state, the reason for jumping?

THE BOX: height, stability, distance from character...

If you have a tendency to go for the spectacular, to think that more is better, then please consider this: master the fundamentals first. Know how to do something in its simplest form so well that you can do it with ease before you even think about adding complexity. Any studio that properly reviews your animation will be more impressed with the basics done extremely well than they will with poorly executed complicated animation.

THE REPETITION OF A TASK IS THE WAY TO MASTER IT.

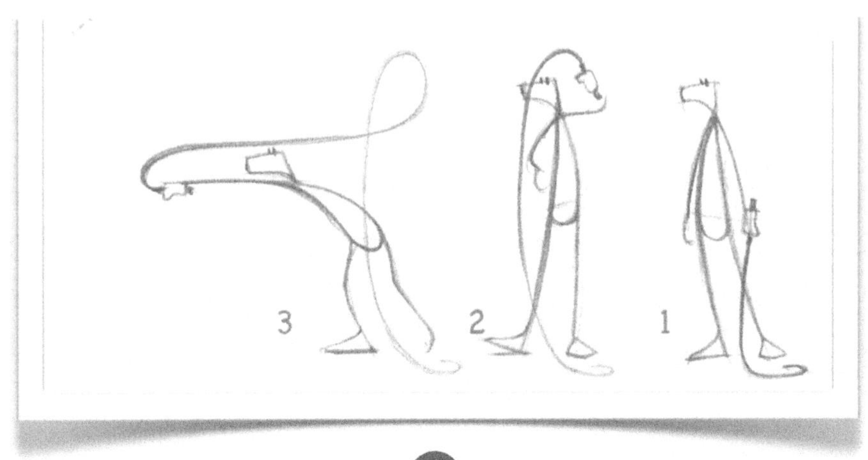

JUMP - LAND - RECOVER

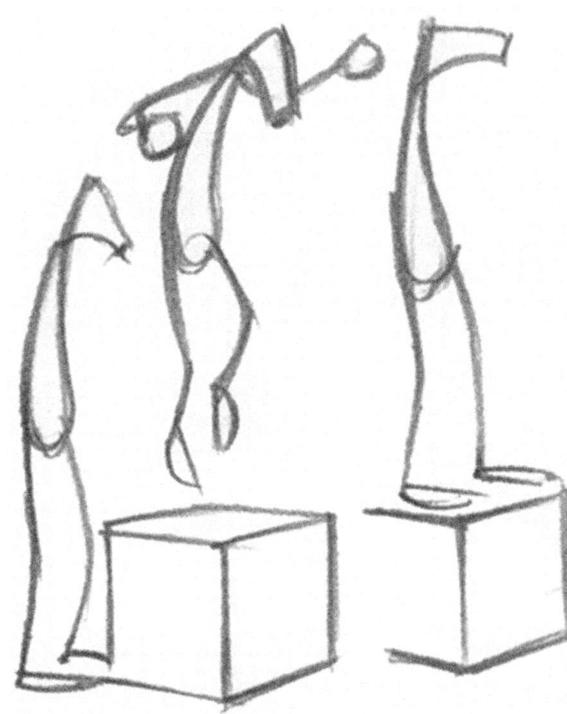

TRY THIS SIMPLE EXERCISE:
(Yah right)

JUMP UP - JUMP DOWN
PLAN EVERY COMPONENT OF
THE EXERCISE WITH AS
MUCH DETAIL AS YOU CAN
THINK OF.

1. Big jump - big force
2. Small drop - small force
3. Small jump - little force
4. Big drop - big force
5. Recovery

ANIMATING AN ACTION
IS MUCH EASIER THAN
ANIMATING THE
RECOVERY FROM AN
ACTION

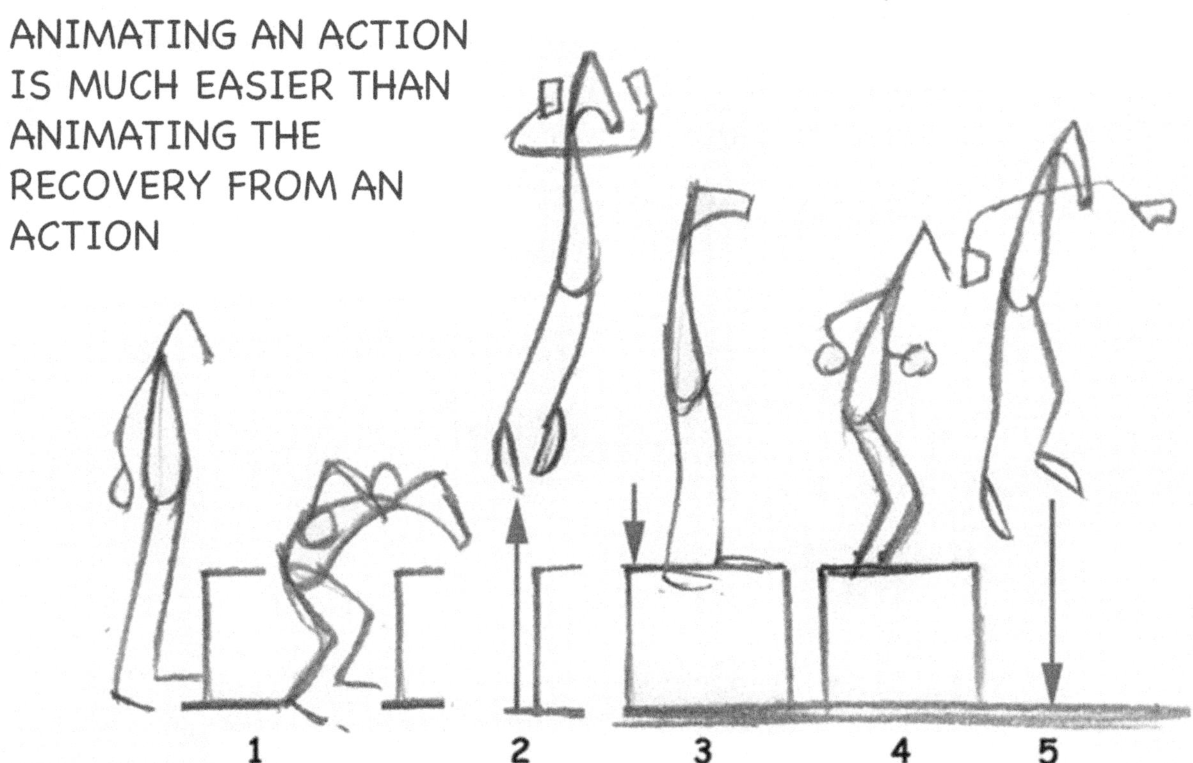

WHAT MOVES FIRST? WHAT FOLLOWS? WHAT WILL THE
PATH OF ACTION BE? HOW HIGH WILL HE JUMP? HOW
MUCH COMPRESSION WILL THERE BE IN RELATION TO EACH
JUMP? WILL HE BE OFF BALANCE WHEN HE LANDS AND IF
YES, HOW WILL HE RECOVER HIS BALANCE - OR WILL HE?

180 DEGREE JUMP AND LAND

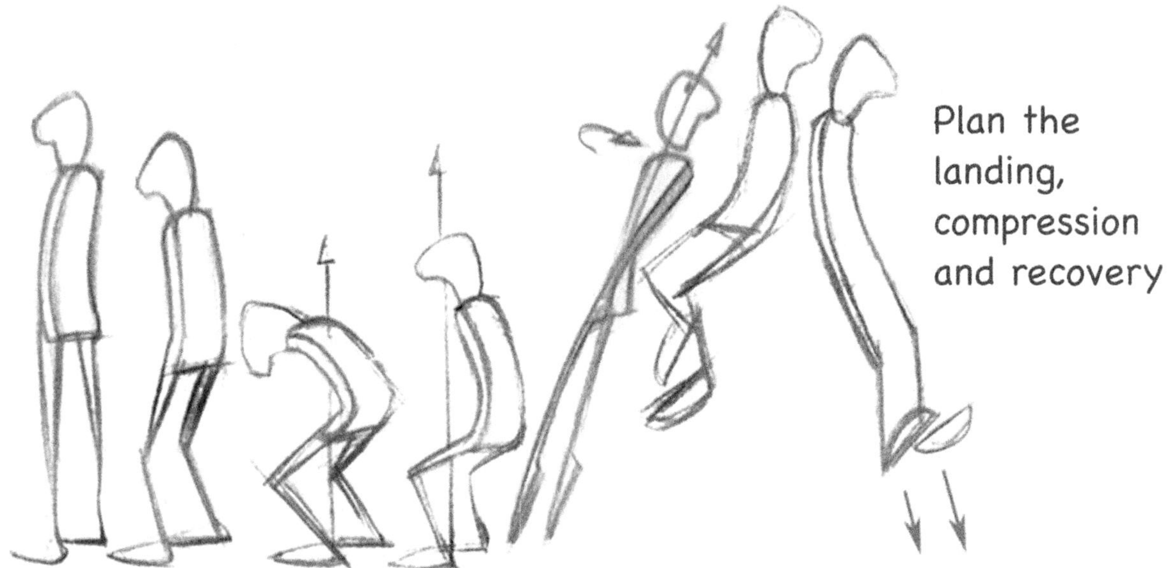

character's posture * compression * lead and follow

The force from both legs drives up through the center of the body mass in the direction of travel - the path of action (POA). The leading twist of the upper body will slow down allowing the legs to take the lead and prepare for compression on landing.

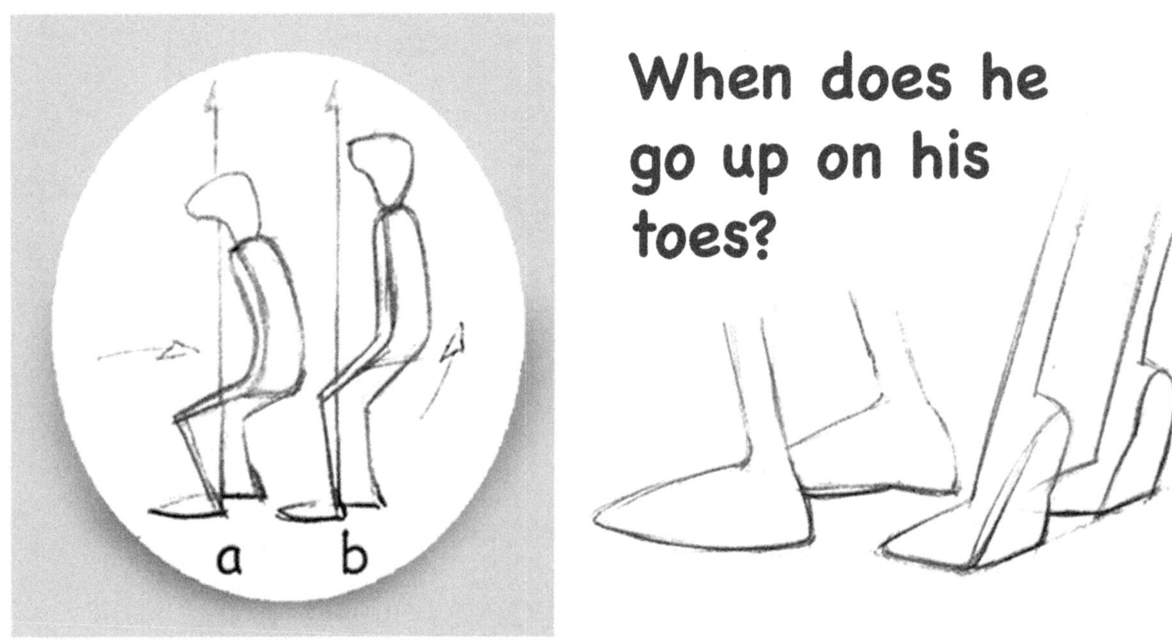

Does he lean back then extend or extend as he leans back?

ANIMATION PLANNING
ROUGH STORYBOARDS

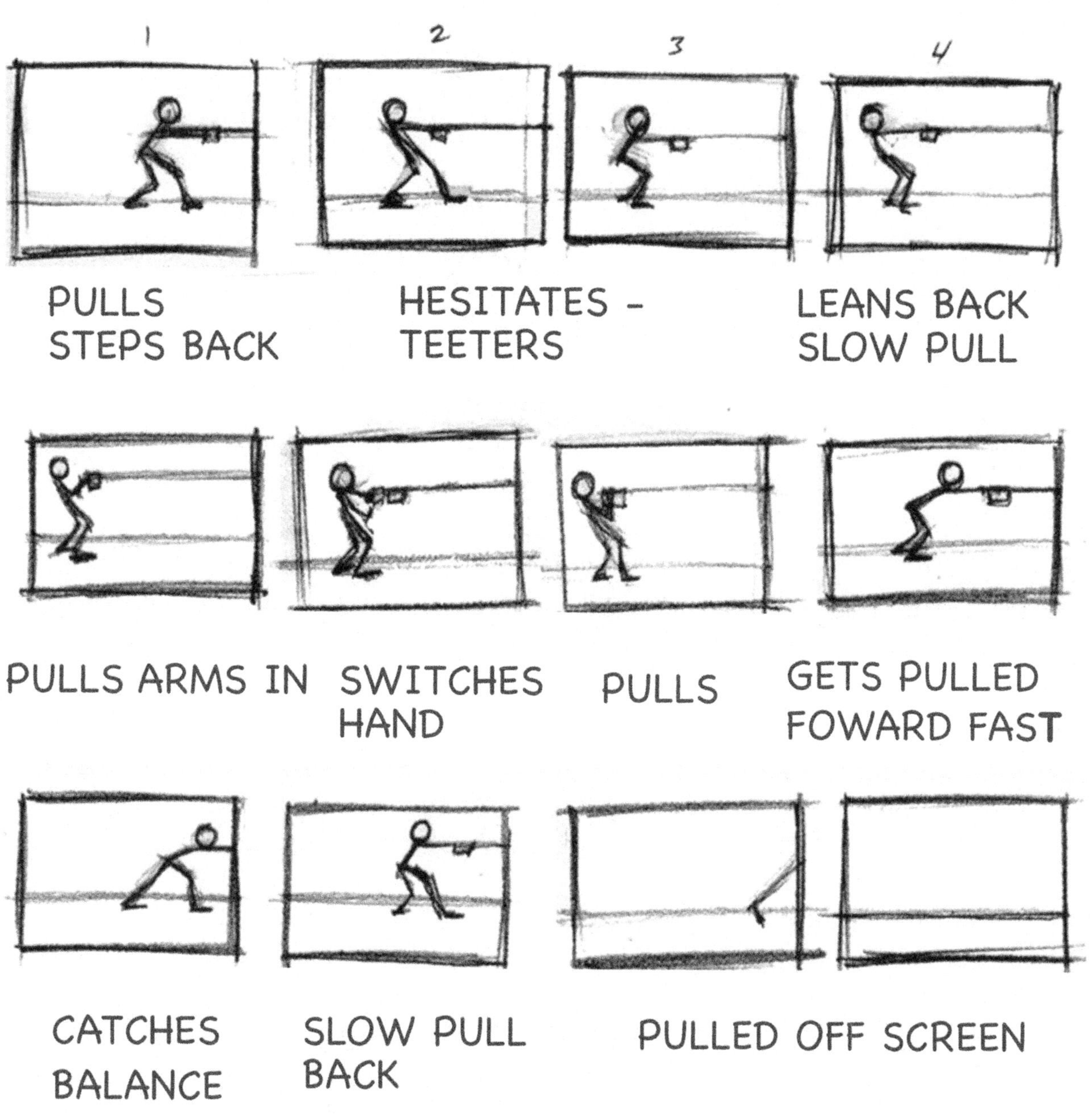

Note panels 5a and 5b – these were added after the original thumbnail boards were done. Planning pages should be rough, often out of order. Once you have all of the necessary information, organize it the way you want it – editing.

ruff storyboards

How drastic is his reaction to the box hitting his hand?

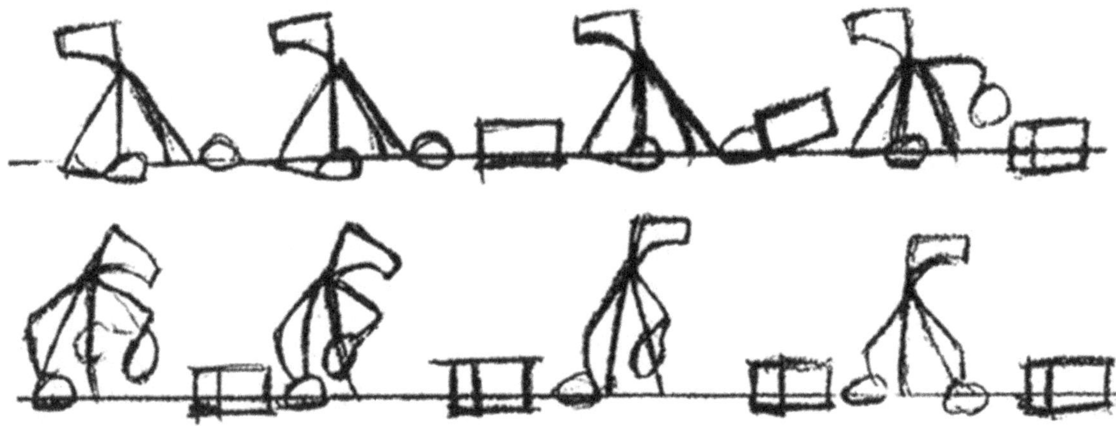

How concerned is he about where it came from?

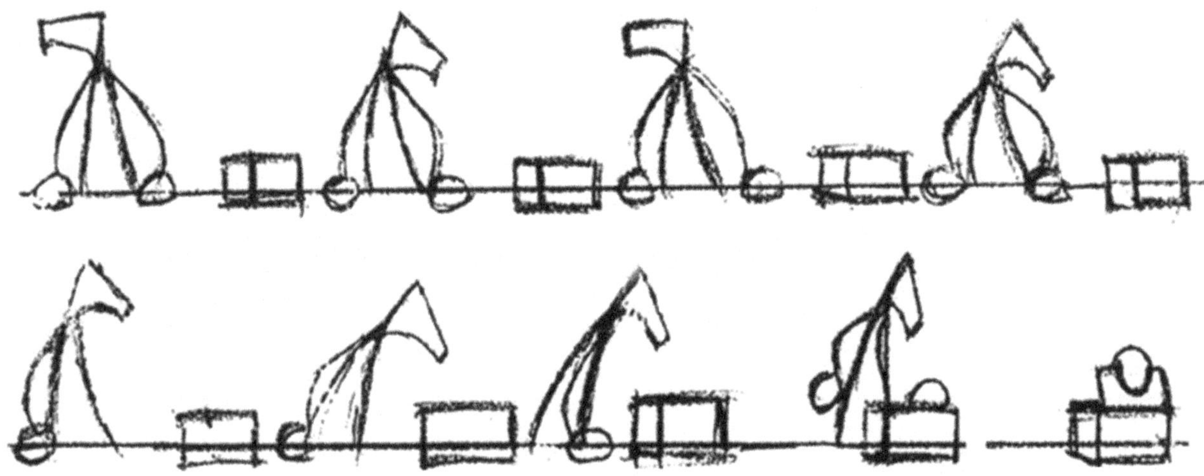

Does he open it ... how cautiously ... what's in it?

Ruff sketches - ideas first. You can use any character design once the planning is complete.

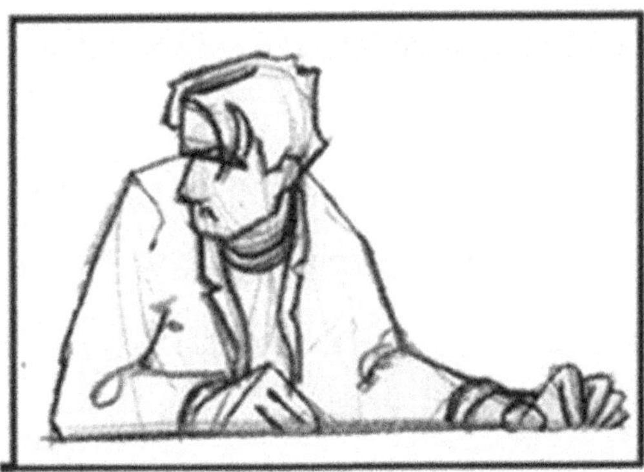

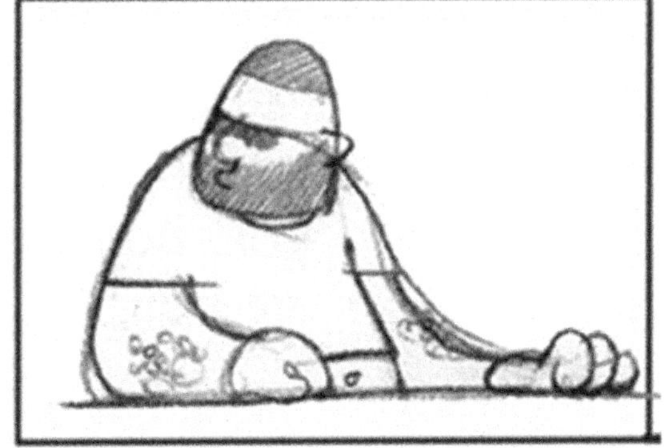

THE HUMAN BODY SIMPLIFIED

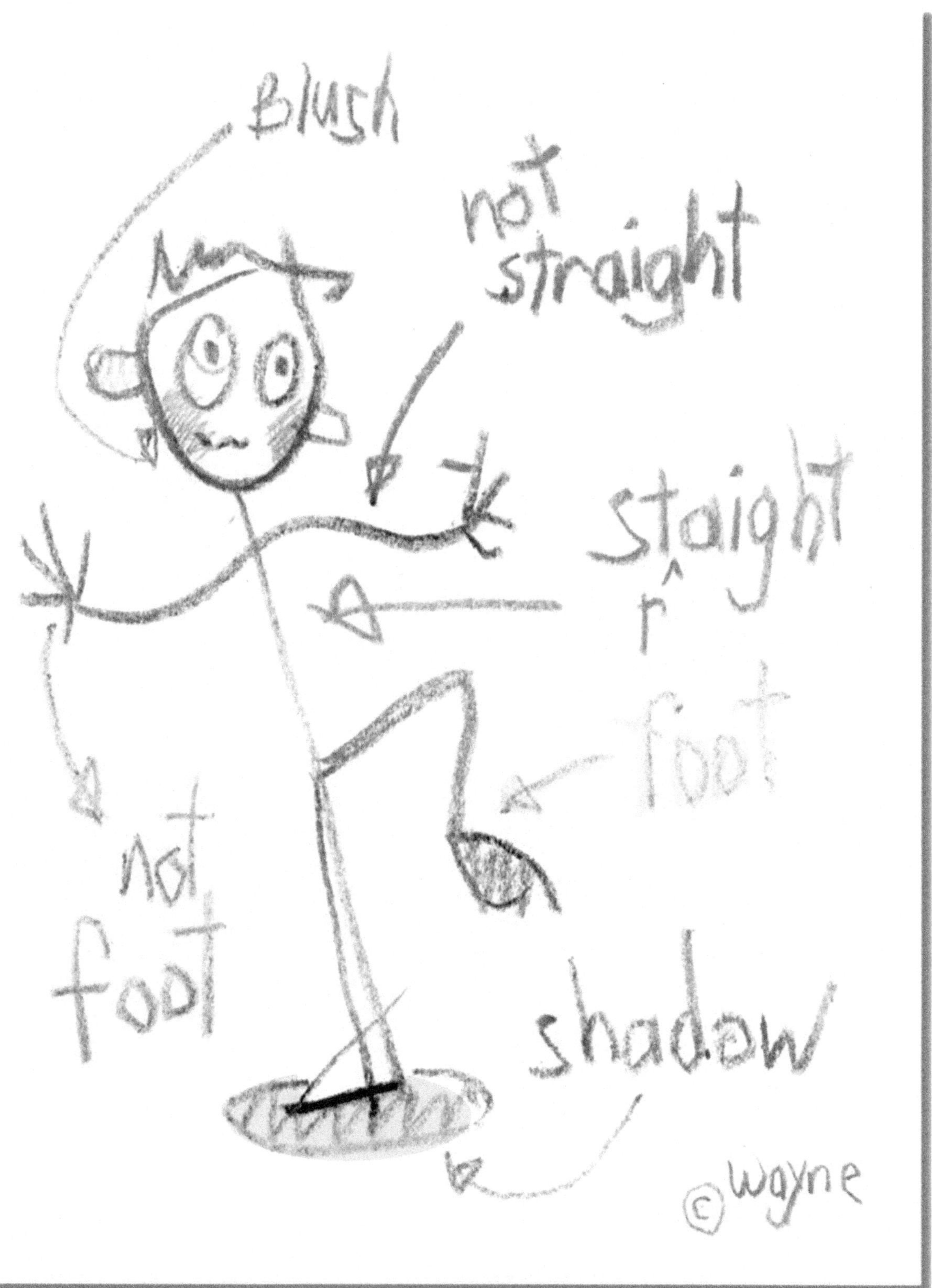

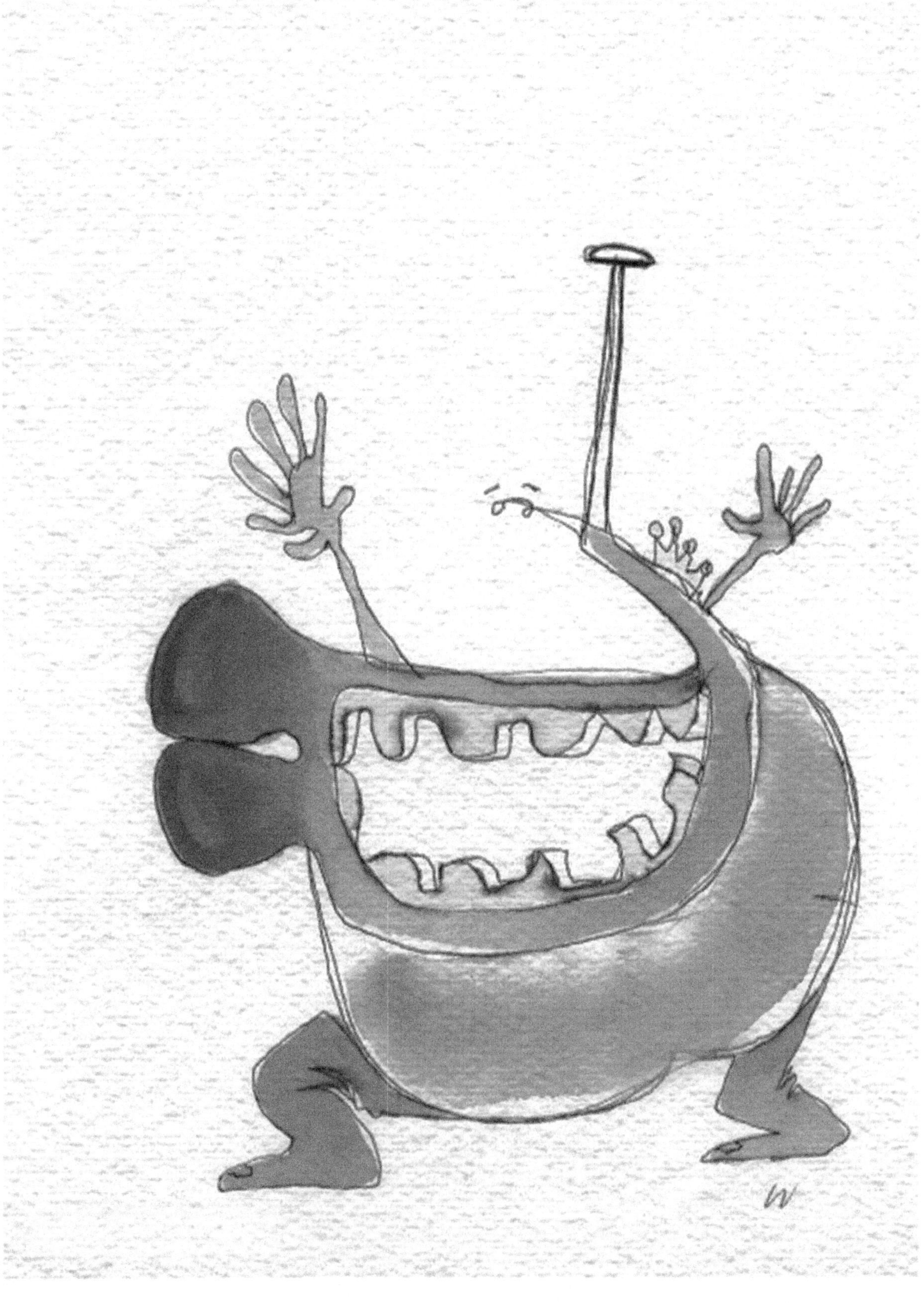

BOOKS

You may already have a number of books on drawing and it is certain that all good books on the subject contain the same information. Often the information is delivered only through drawings and too much is left for us to figure out on our own. In Burne Hogarth's books, he supports the visual content with amazingly clear text. **DYNAMIC FIGURE DRAWING**, by Burne Hogarth is the most highly recommended book for clear information that will help you learn to draw the human form.

The Torso
Dynamic Figure Drawing - Burne Hogarth
Pages 21, 22, 44-47, 55
George Bridgman's Life Drawing - George Bridgman
Pages 22-33
Atlas of Human Anatomy for the Artist - Peck
Pages 32,33, 38

Legs and Feet
Dynamic Figure Drawing - Burne Hogarth
Legs pages 30-40, 48-54, 156. Feet pages 37-40
George Bridgman's Life Drawing - George Bridgman
160-169
Atlas of Human Anatomy for the Artist - Peck
Pages 134-143

ARMS and HANDS - shoulder, elbow, wrist
Dynamic Figure Drawing - Burne Hogarth
Arms pages 26-30, 55-58, 136
Hands pages 37, 120-124
Drawing Dynamic Hands - Burne Hogarth
George Bridgman's Life Drawing - George Bridgman
Pages 148-158
Atlas of Human Anatomy for the Artist - Peck
Pages 114-127

Neck and Head
Dynamic Figure Drawing - Burne Hogarth

Drawing the Human Head - Burne Hogarth
Pages 59, 60, 91-94
George Bridgman's Life Drawing - George Bridgman
Pages 95-133
Atlas of Human Anatomy for the Artist - Peck
Pages 10-20

FULL BODY - three simplified versions of human form
Dynamic Figure Drawing - Burne Hogarth pages 44, 51, 55
George Bridgman's Life Drawing - page.31
Atlas of Human Anatomy for the Artist - Peck page 195

Exercise: Choose a few pictures from your favourite artist
or book on life drawing; take a cartoon character and draw
them in the same poses. This is an exercise used in Drawing
for Animation class at college.

There may be many books that you are more comfortable
with, which is good. The information does not change, use
your choice of reference along with the exercises in this
book.

Highly recommended books:
Dynamic Figure Drawing - Burne Hogarth
Basic Principles of Design - Manfred Maier
The Natural Way to Draw - Kimon Niclolaides
The Art of Perspective Drawing - The Grumbacher Library

Animators do not have the luxury of drawing only what they
see, they have to draw from knowledge and creativity.

SIMPLIFIED HUMAN ANATOMY

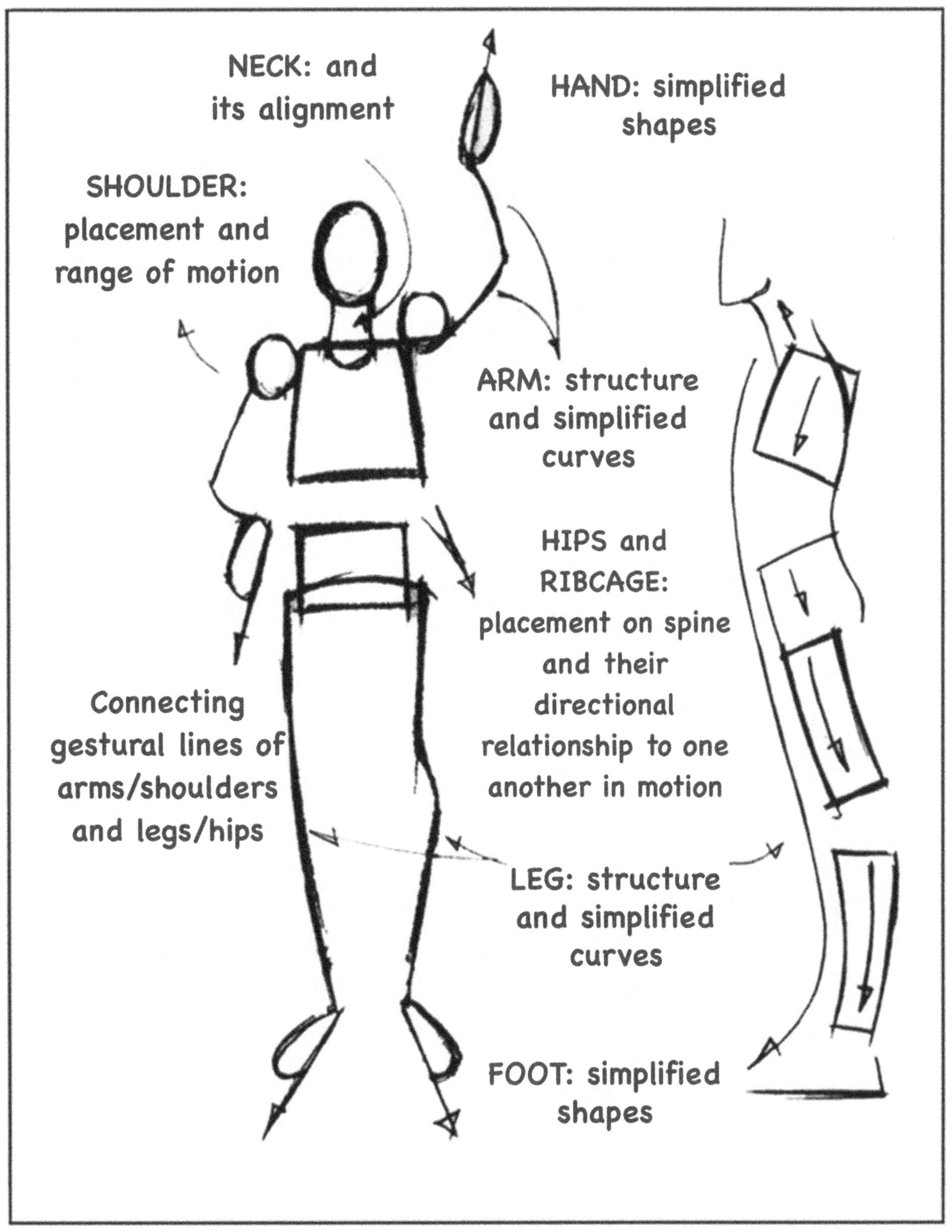

This is what you must know, to confidently simplify your drawings when planning and animating.

THE TORSO

The angles of the rib cage and hips are created by where they are connected to the spine, as is the angle of the neck.

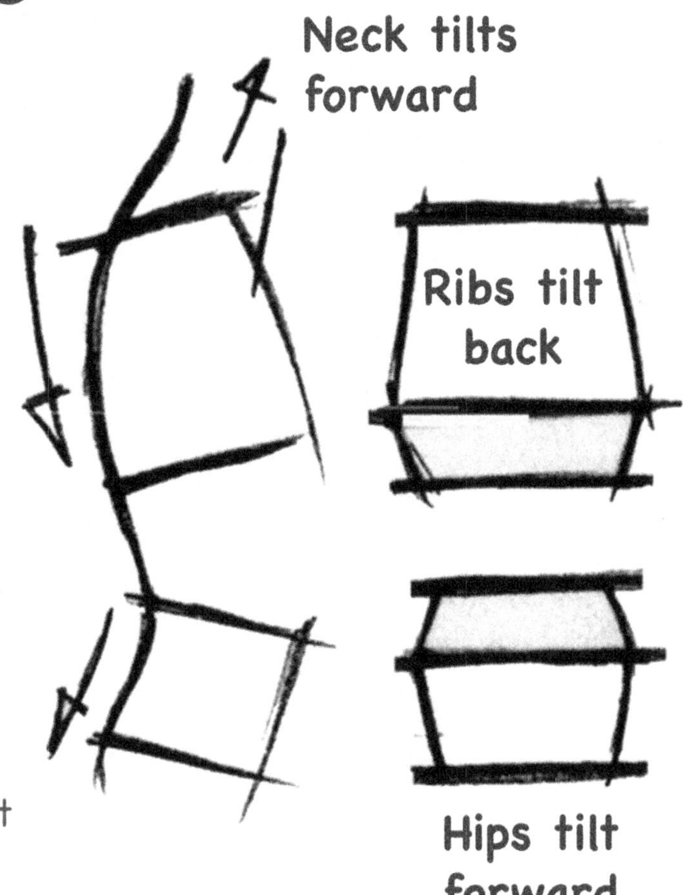

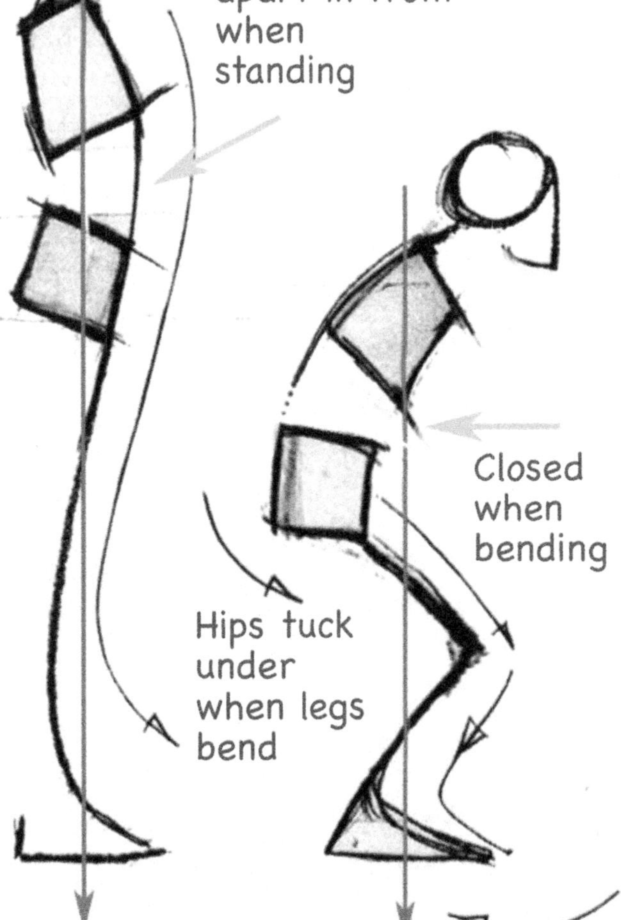

Body sections are not stacked straight over one another. Posture is created by the curvature of the spine, the bending of the legs, how the shoulders are held, the angle of the neck...

Body adjusts over the center of balance when we crouch

TORSO IN 3D

Approach this as a connect the corners game. Draw a line for the shoulders and one for the hips and connect right to right and left to left sides. The detail of realistic shapes will be easier to add after you draw the underlying structure.

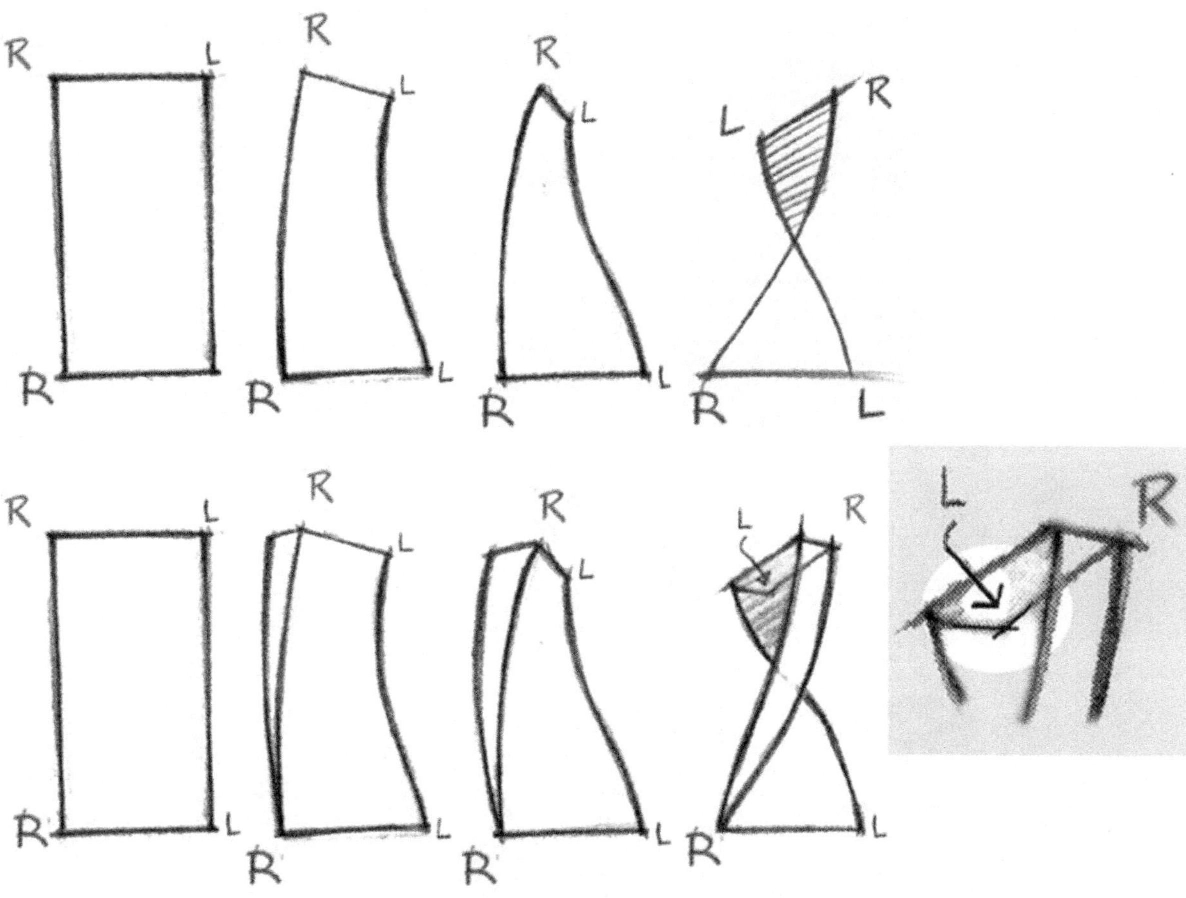

Learning how to draw the torso in 3D is very important for animating twist and torque. Twisting a body or an object creates tension or built-up force. This is essential for animating with lead and follow. The upper body can turn first and pull the hips around or vice versa.

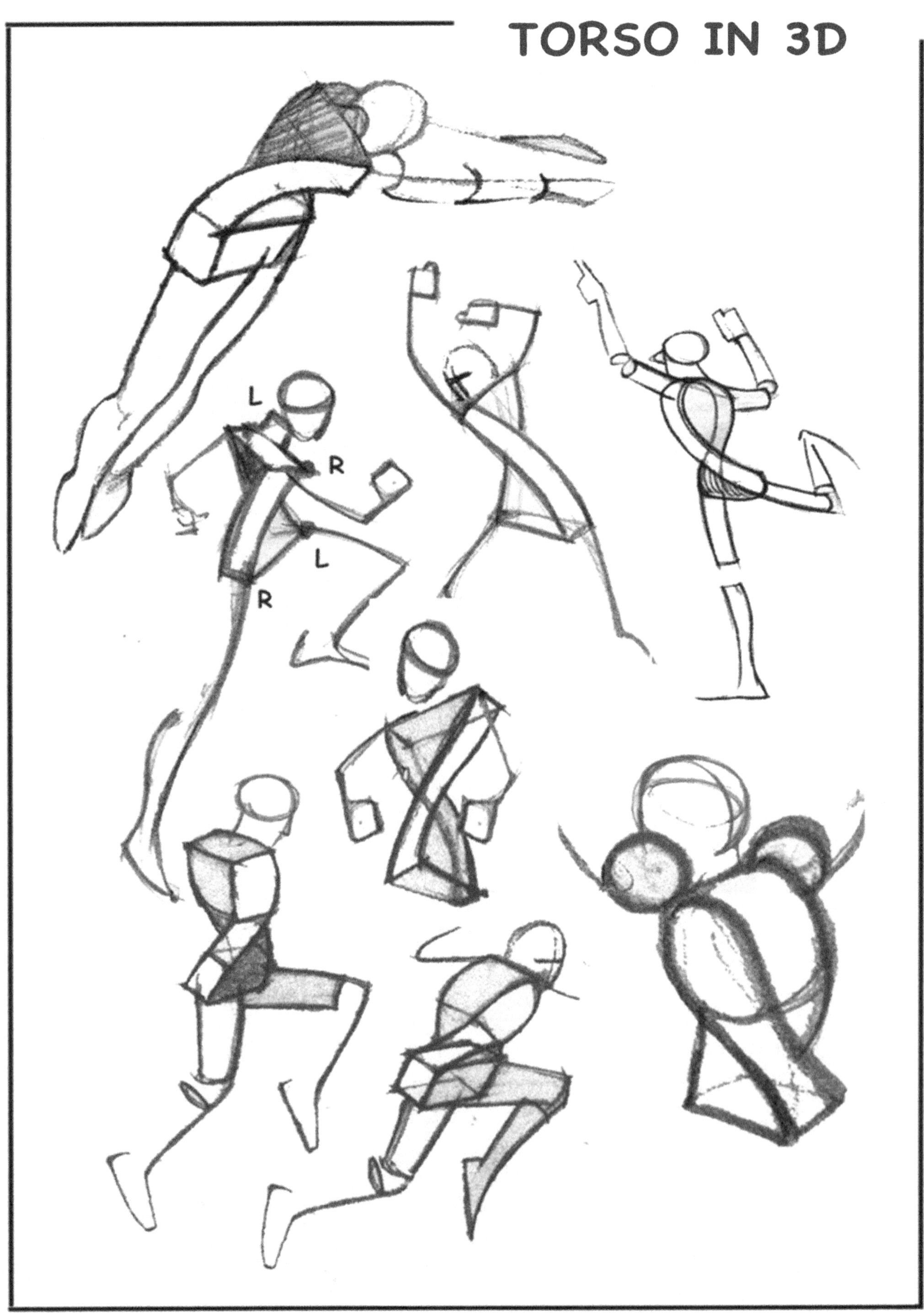

L
R
L
R

SIMPLIFIED LEGS

FRONT:

1   2   3   4   5

THE UPPER LEG IS ONE SIMPLE CYLINDER THAT CURVES FROM HIP TO KNEE

THE UPPER AND LOWER LEG ARE OFFSET AT THE KNEE

THE LOWER LEG IS ONE SIMPLE CYLINDER THAT CURVES FROM KNEE TO ANKLE AND IS THINNER AT THE ANKLE

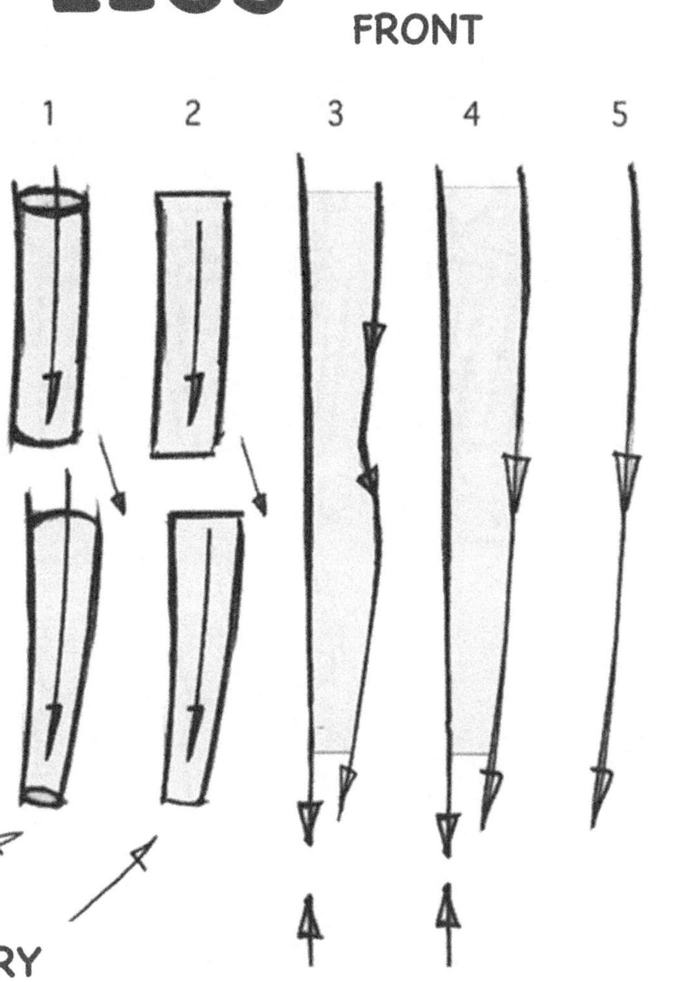

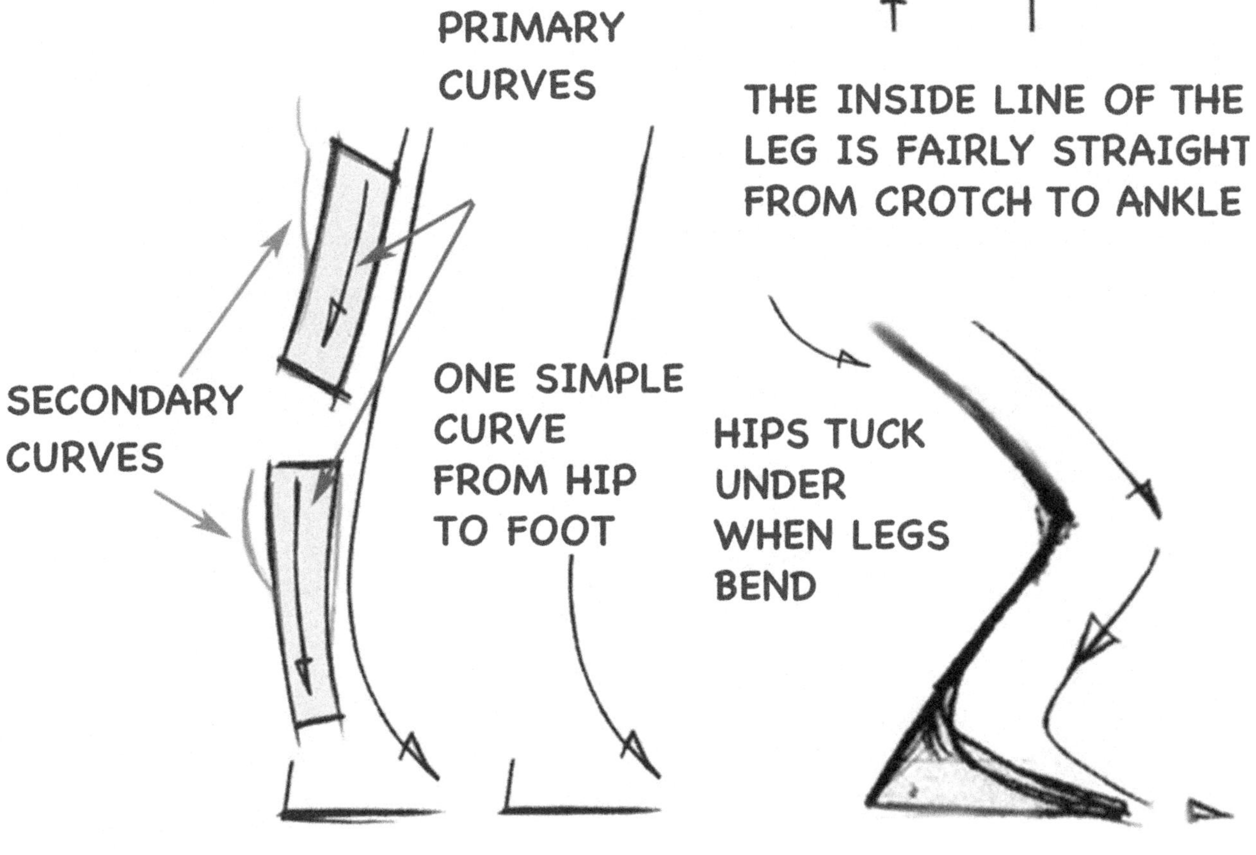

PRIMARY CURVES

THE INSIDE LINE OF THE LEG IS FAIRLY STRAIGHT FROM CROTCH TO ANKLE

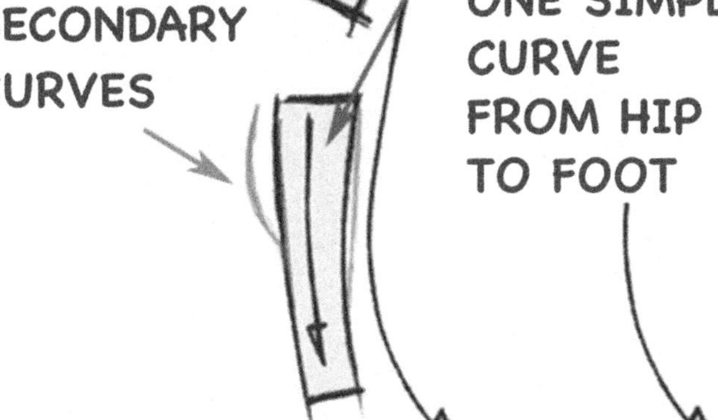

SECONDARY CURVES

ONE SIMPLE CURVE FROM HIP TO FOOT

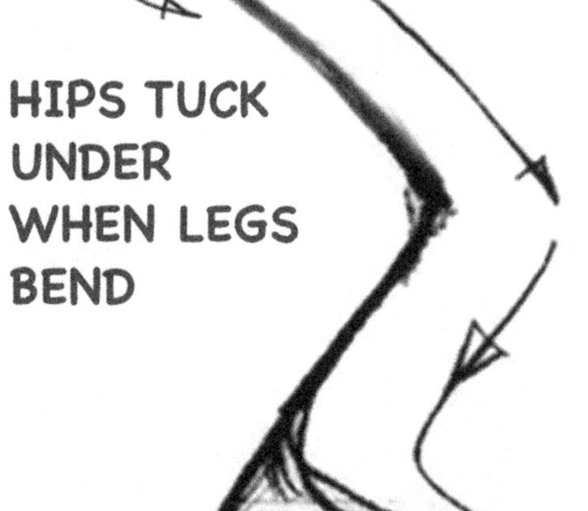

HIPS TUCK UNDER WHEN LEGS BEND

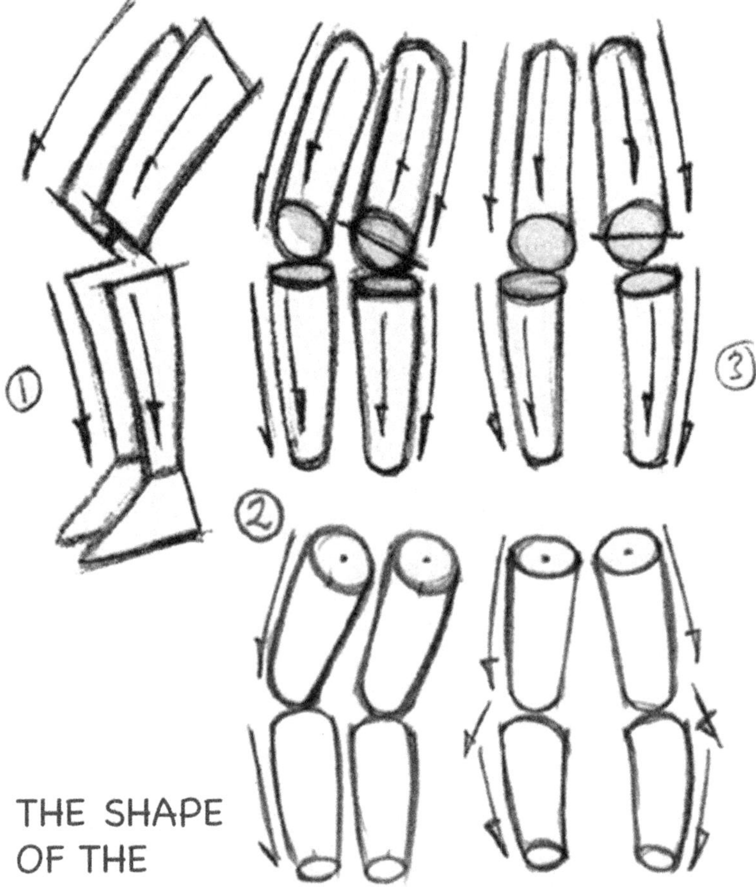

LOOK FOR THE STRUCTURAL CURVES IN ALL OF YOUR DRAWINGS NO MATTER WHAT STYLE YOU TRY. DRAW WITH SOLID STRUCTURE BASED ON SIMPLE SHAPES.

THE SHAPE OF THE LOWER LEG AT THE 3/4 VIEW (#2) IS NEARLY SYMMETRICAL AND LACKS A DOMINANT CURVE

BACK:
REVERSE THE PERSPECTIVE OF THE CYLINDERS BUT THE CURVES STAY THE SAME

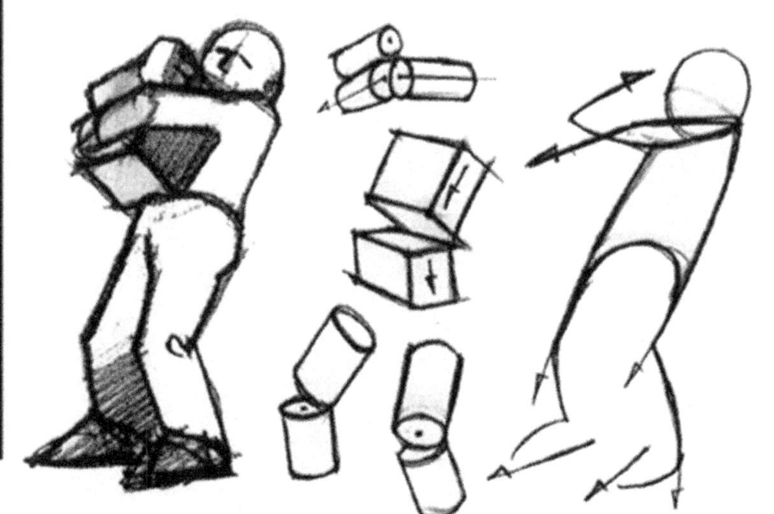

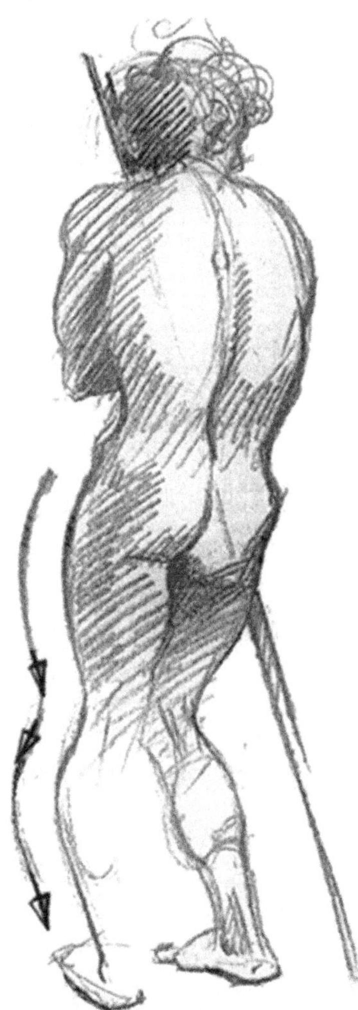

SIMPLIFIED FOOT

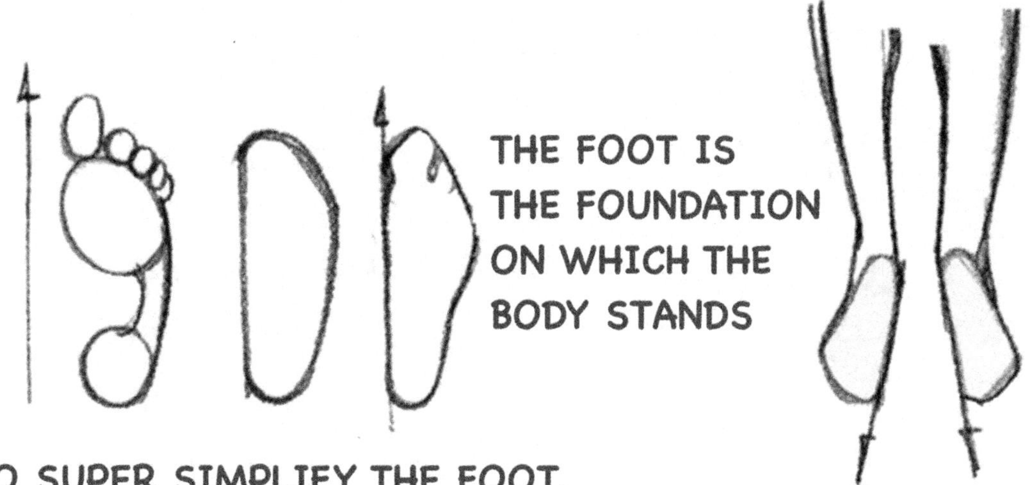

TO SUPER SIMPLIFY THE FOOT, DRAW A STRAIGHT LINE THAT REPRESENTS THE INSIDE OF THE FOOT FROM HEEL TO BIG TOE

EVEN WHEN STANDING ON TOES, THE INSIDE OF THE FOOT CAN BE DRAWN WITH A STRAIGHT LINE

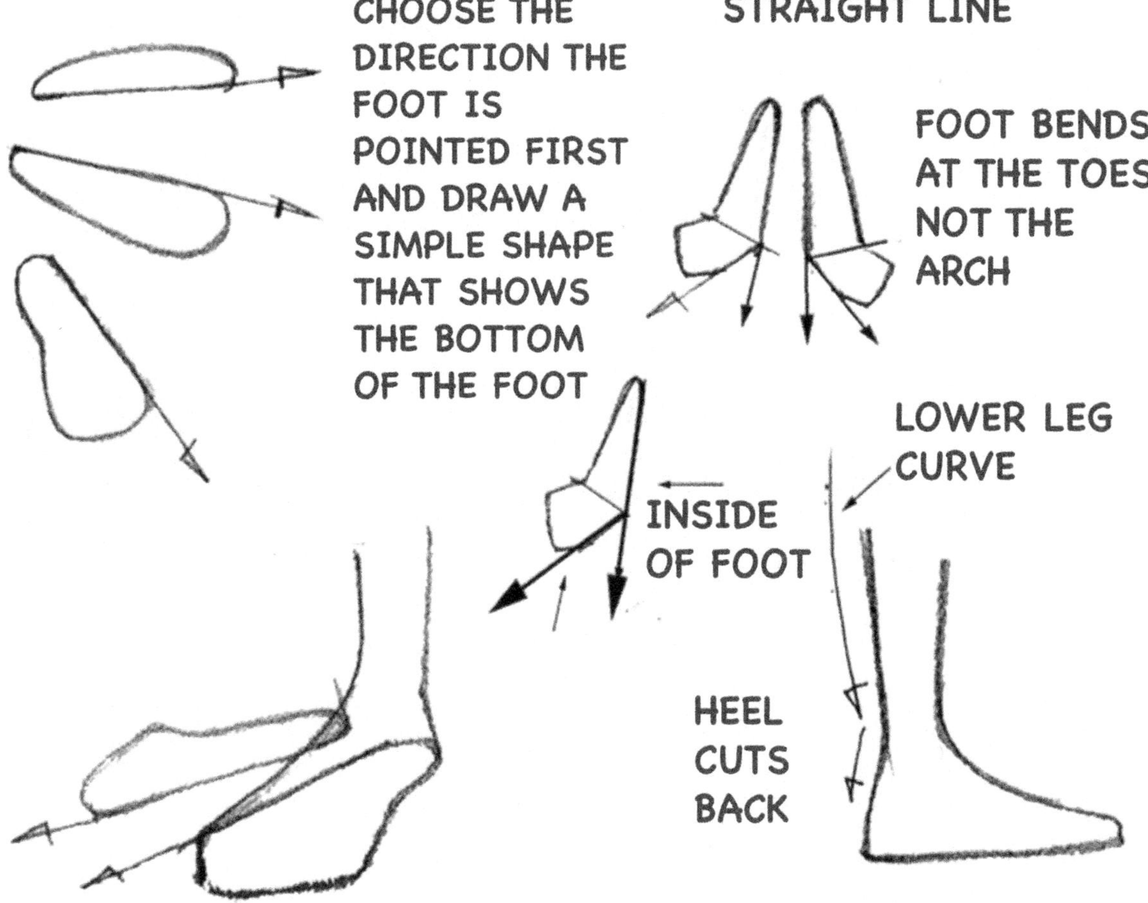

SIMPLIFIED HANDS

FIRST DRAW THE PALM OR BACK OF THE HAND AND HOW IT LINES UP WITH THE FOREARM.

SLIGHTLY NARROWED AT THE WRIST

THE DIRECTIONAL RELATIONSHIP OF THE FOREARM AND INDEX FINGER WILL ALMOST ALWAYS CAPTURE THE GESTURE OR ESSENCE OF THE POSE

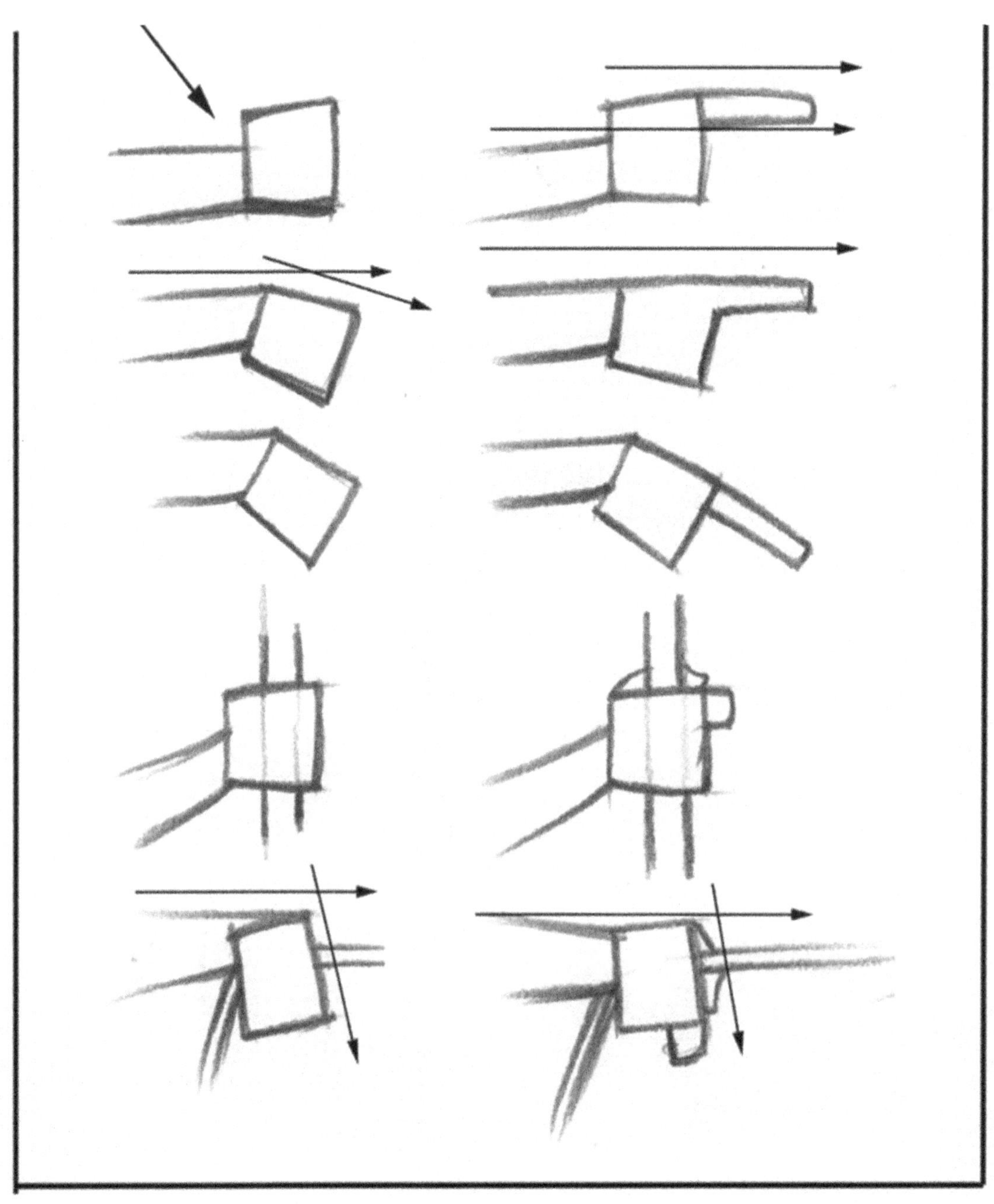

SIMPLIFIED HANDS

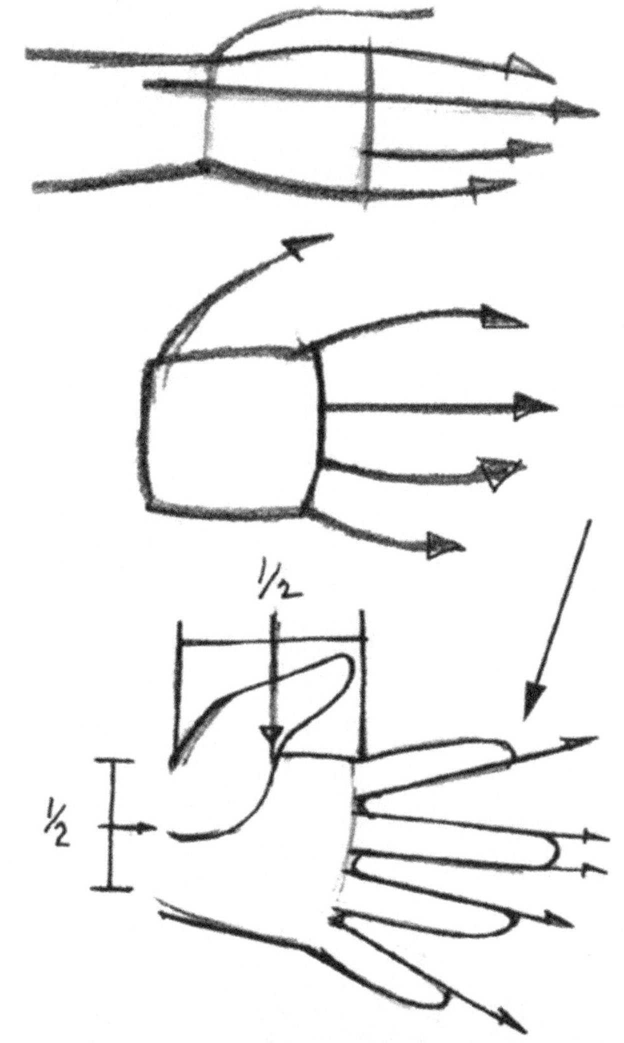

HANDS CAN BE VERY EXPRESSIVE WITHOUT DETAIL

TRY THIS GUIDE:
*THE MIDDLE FINGER IS STRAIGHT, THE OTHER FINGERS GENTLY CURVE TOWARD IT.

*TO AVOID OVER CURVING - DRAW THE INSIDE EDGE STRAIGHT AND THE OUTSIDE EDGE WITH A SLIGHT CURVE AND TAPER TO THE FINGER TIP

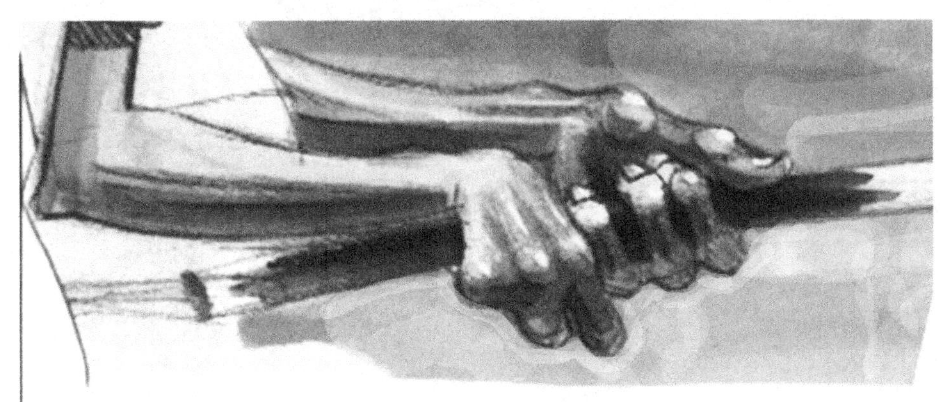

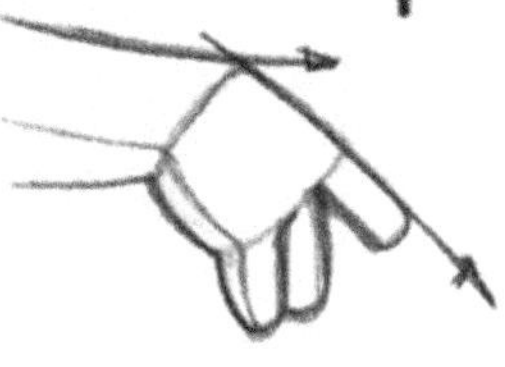

SIMPLIFIED HANDS

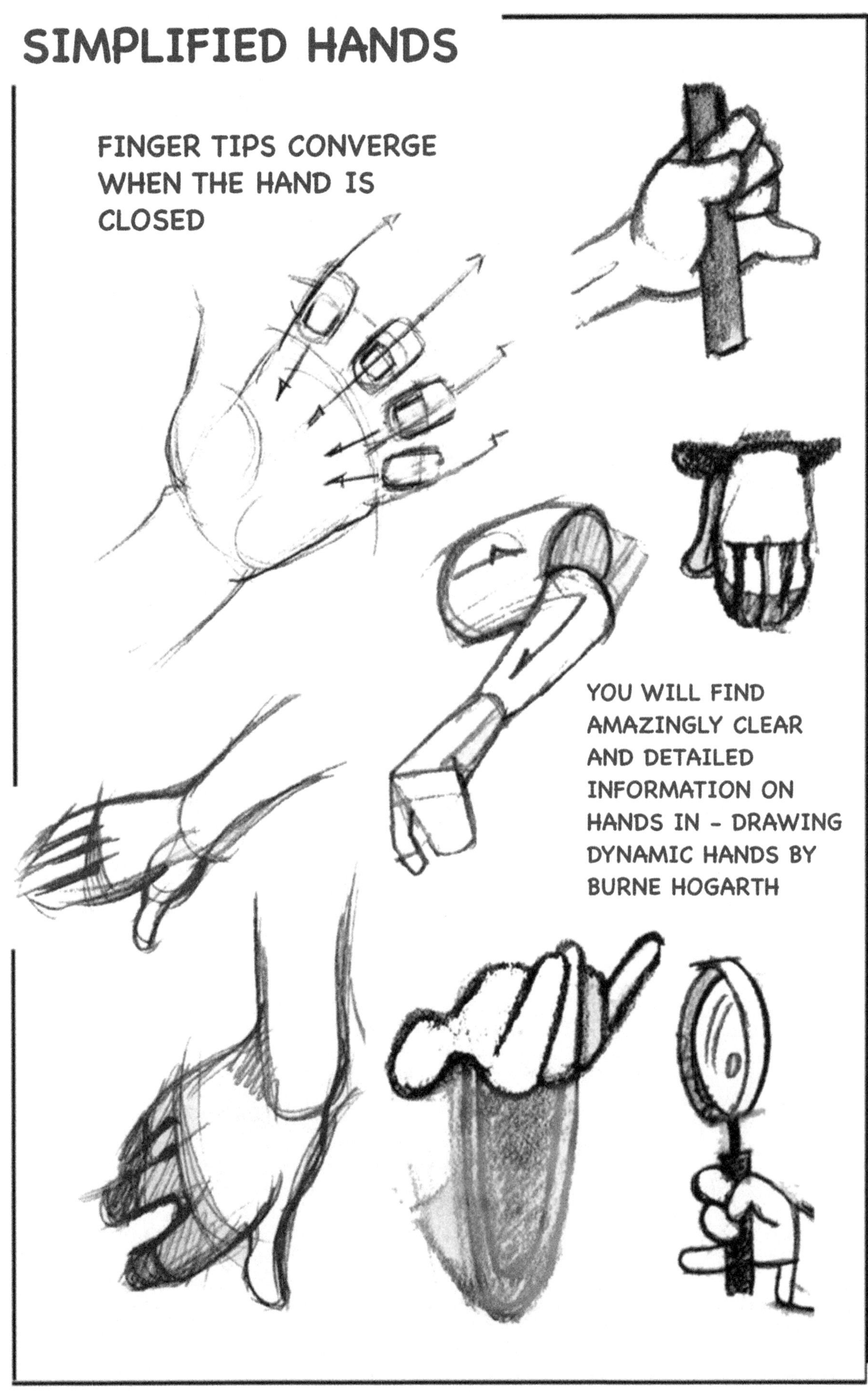

FINGER TIPS CONVERGE
WHEN THE HAND IS
CLOSED

YOU WILL FIND
AMAZINGLY CLEAR
AND DETAILED
INFORMATION ON
HANDS IN - DRAWING
DYNAMIC HANDS BY
BURNE HOGARTH

SIMPLIFIED ARM CURVES

THE ARM HAS TWO
SLIGHTLY CURVED
CYLINDERS - UPPER
AND LOWER ARM

THERE IS ONE
SIMPLE FLOW-THROUGH
CURVE RUNNING
FROM
ARMPIT
TO WRIST
AT THE BACK
OF THE ARM

THE BICEP AND FOREARM
MUSCLES ARE SECONDARY
CURVES AND SHORTER IN LENGTH
THAN THE MAJOR TRICEP CURVE -
DON'T USE SECONDARY CURVES
TO SIMPLIFY THE ARM

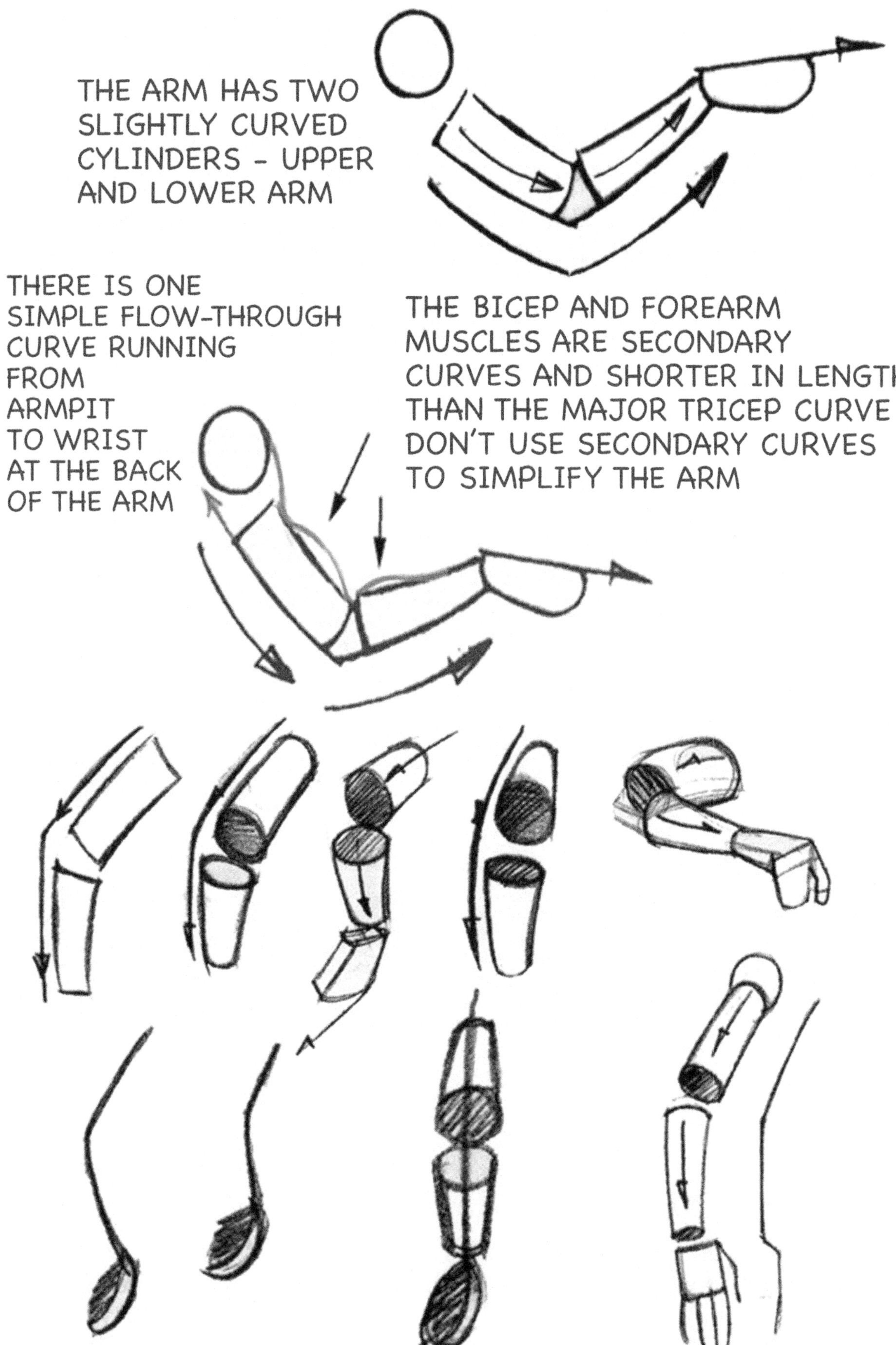

SHOULDERS HAVE A HUGE RANGE OF MOTION. SHOW THAT MOTION IN YOUR DRAWINGS AND ANIMATION

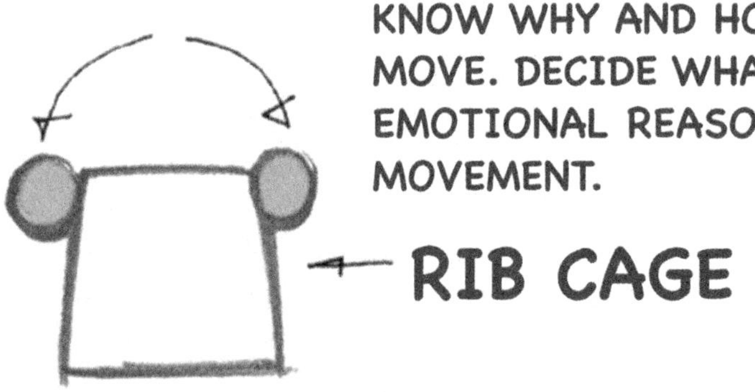

KNOW WHY AND HOW THE SHOULDERS MOVE. DECIDE WHAT THE PHYSICAL AND EMOTIONAL REASONS ARE FOR THAT MOVEMENT.

RIB CAGE

SHOULDERS CAN MOVE IN ALL DIRECTIONS. THEY CAN BE PULLED DOWN BY THE WEIGHT OF AN OBJECT OR EMOTIONAL SADNESS.

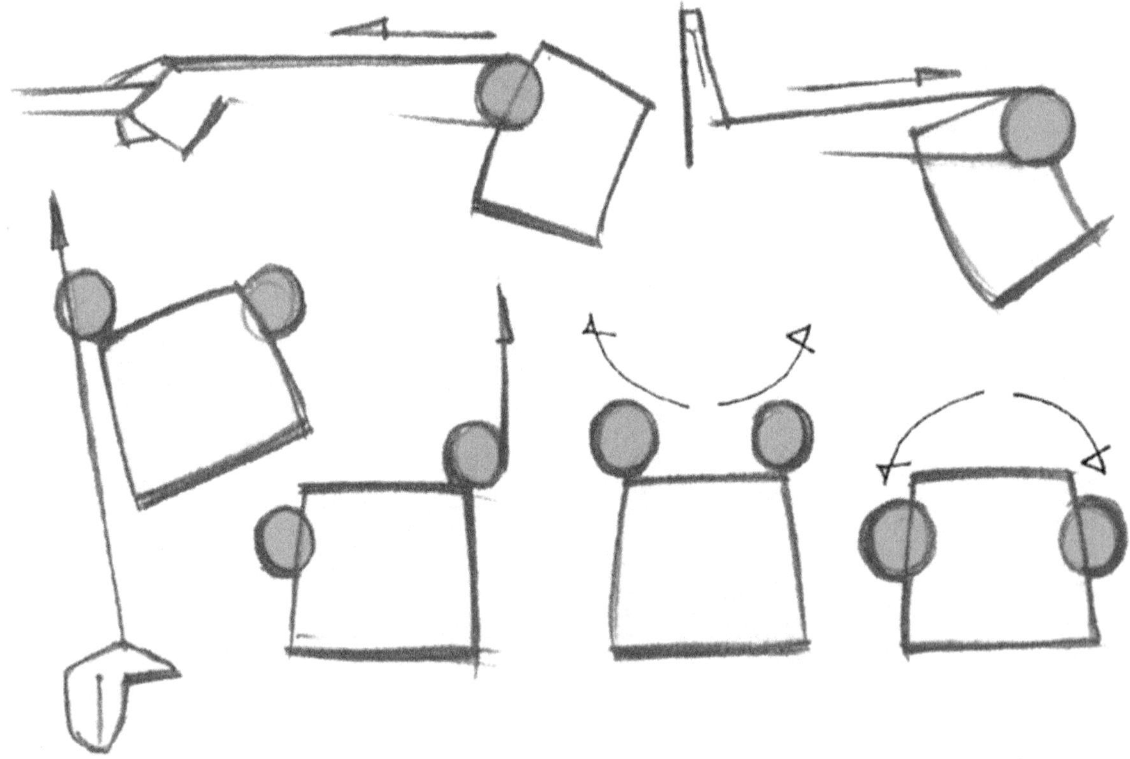

YOUR SHOULDER IS THE FIRST TO MOVE WHEN YOU RAISE YOUR HAND OVER YOUR HEAD - TRY IT, FEEL IT, UNDERSTAND IT.

THE SIMPLIFIED HEAD

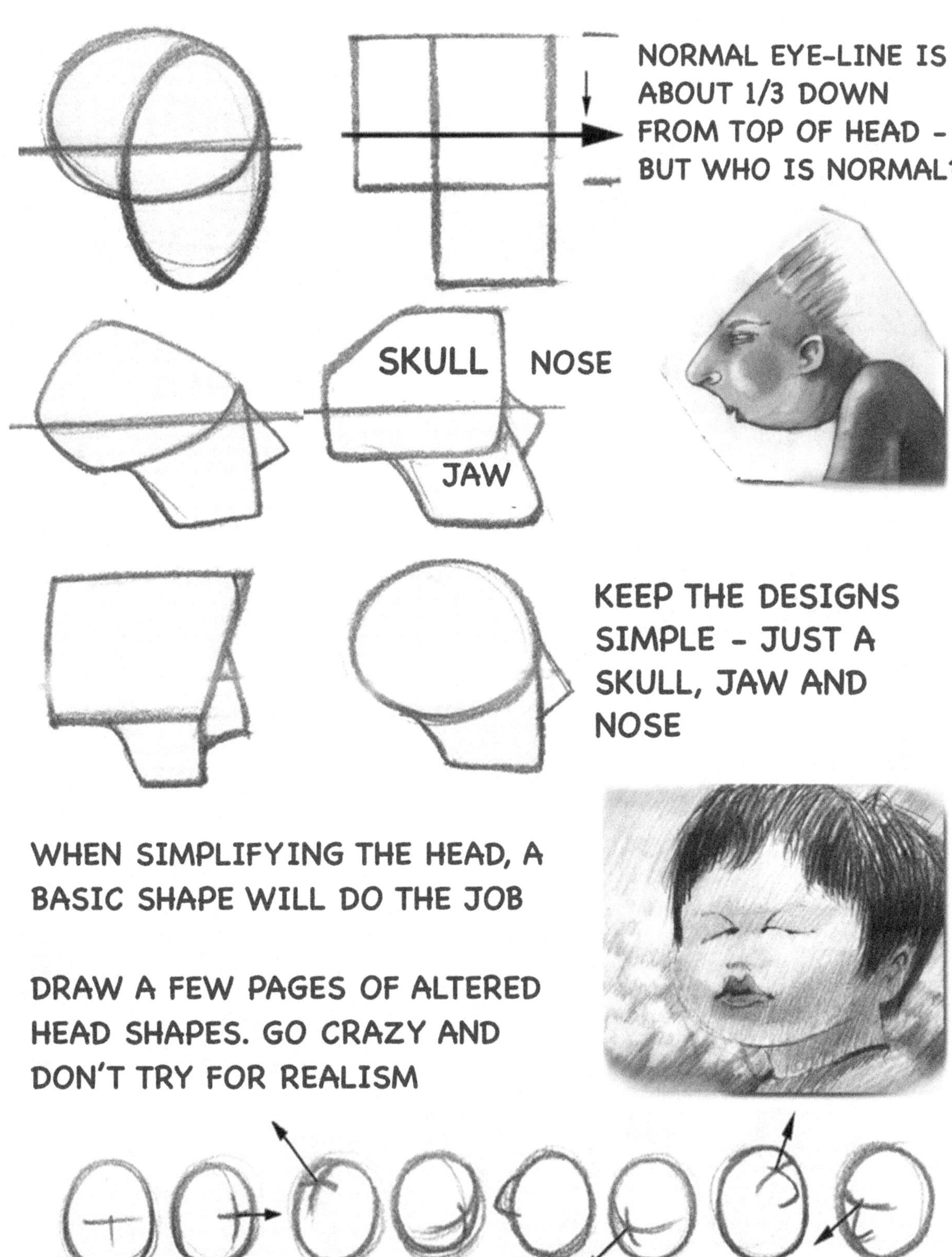

NORMAL EYE-LINE IS ABOUT 1/3 DOWN FROM TOP OF HEAD - BUT WHO IS NORMAL?

KEEP THE DESIGNS SIMPLE - JUST A SKULL, JAW AND NOSE

WHEN SIMPLIFYING THE HEAD, A BASIC SHAPE WILL DO THE JOB

DRAW A FEW PAGES OF ALTERED HEAD SHAPES. GO CRAZY AND DON'T TRY FOR REALISM

FOR BASIC PLANNING AND SIMPLICITY OF DESIGN, JUST DRAW A CIRCLE AND CROSS HAIR LINES THAT INDICATE EYE DIRECTION AND THE CENTER OF THE HEAD

WHAT DOES A BOXER'S FACE LOOK LIKE?

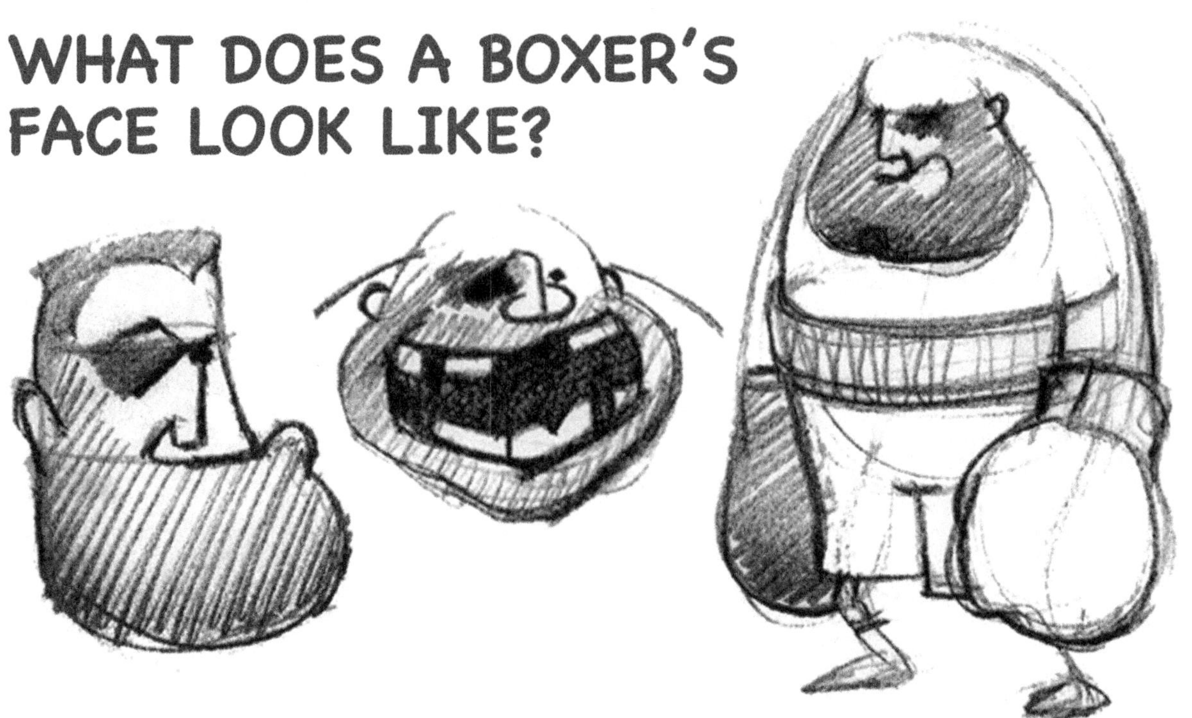

DRAW A BUNCH OF BASIC SHAPES AND PLACE THE EYES HIGH, MID, LOW, FAR APART - PLAY WITH DESIGN.

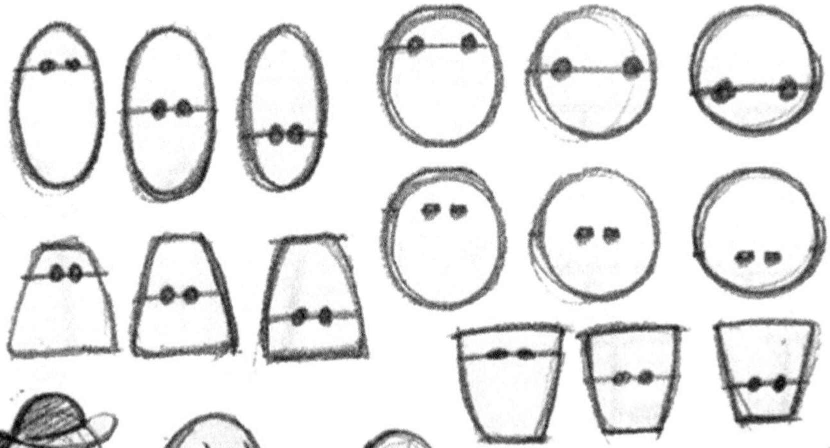

DRAW UNTIL YOU CAPTURE THE ESSENCE OF THE DESIGN YOU WANT BEFORE ADDING DETAILS.

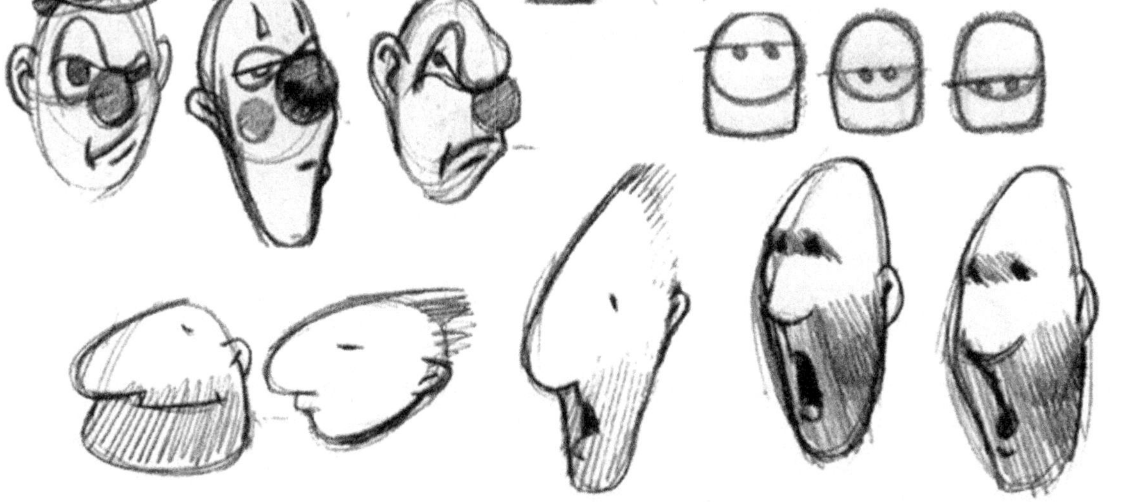

PLAY with shapes that are based on the structural information in this section and in the books listed earlier.

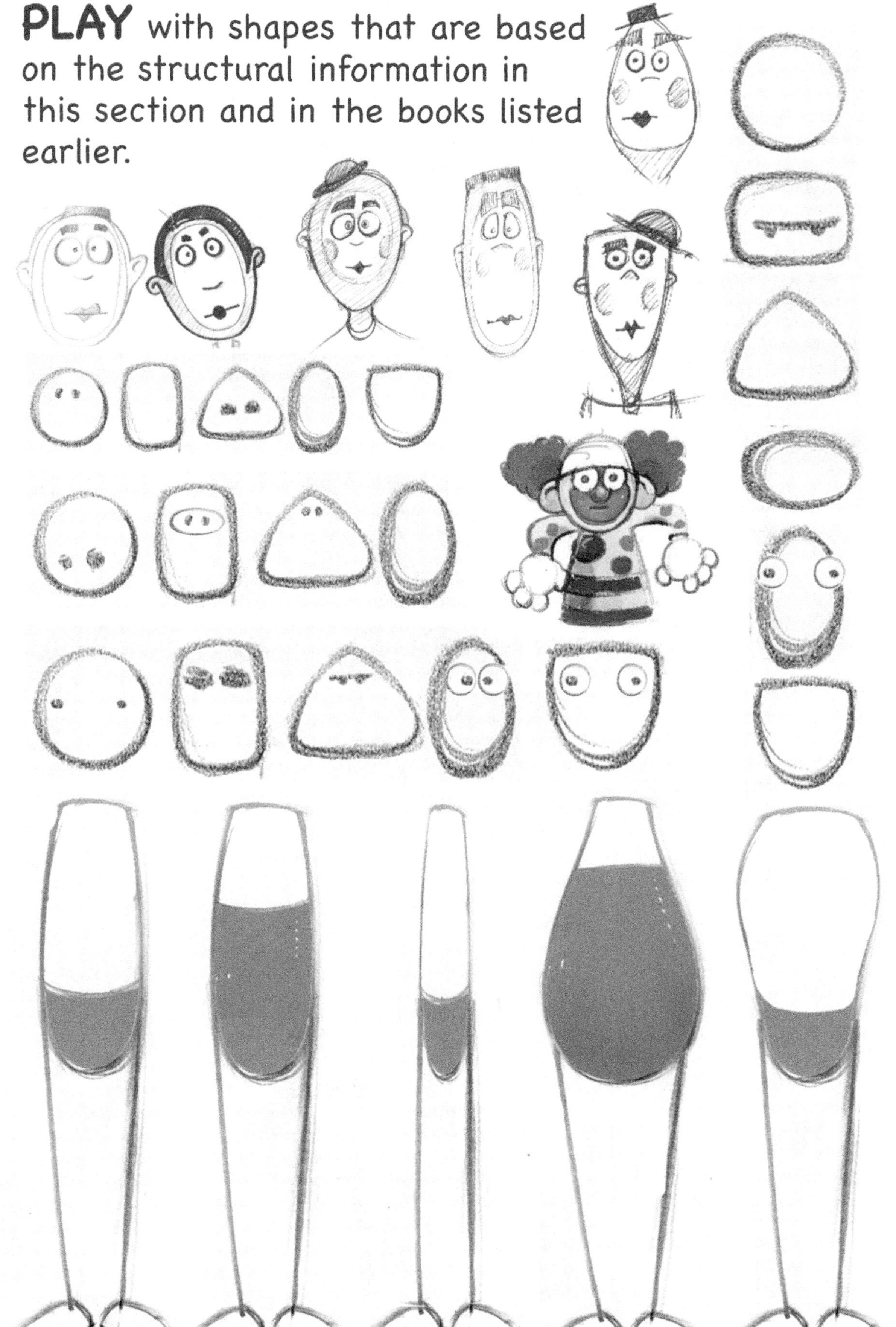

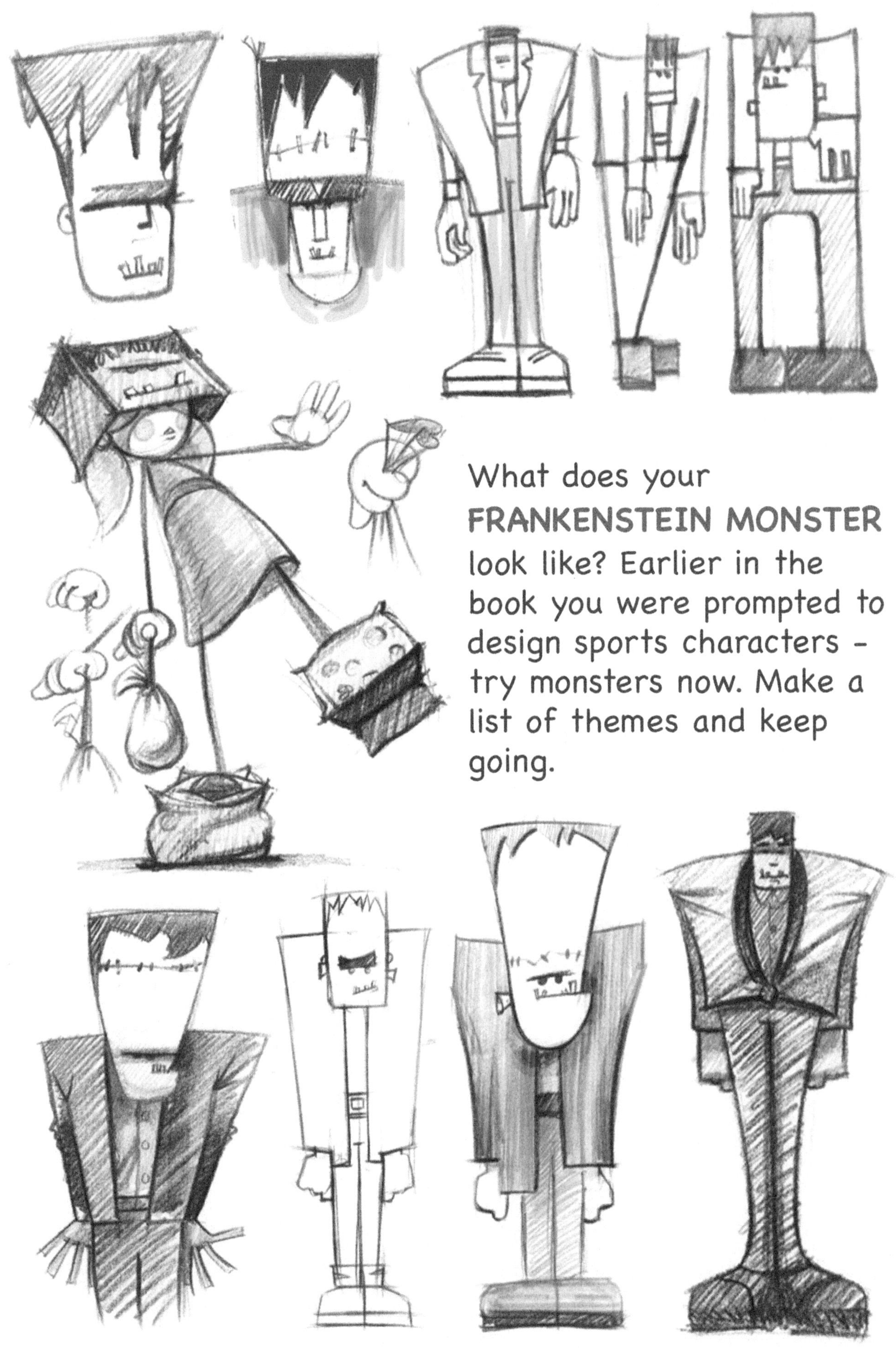

What does your **FRANKENSTEIN MONSTER** look like? Earlier in the book you were prompted to design sports characters - try monsters now. Make a list of themes and keep going.

CENTER OF GRAVITY, BALANCE AND BODY SECTIONS

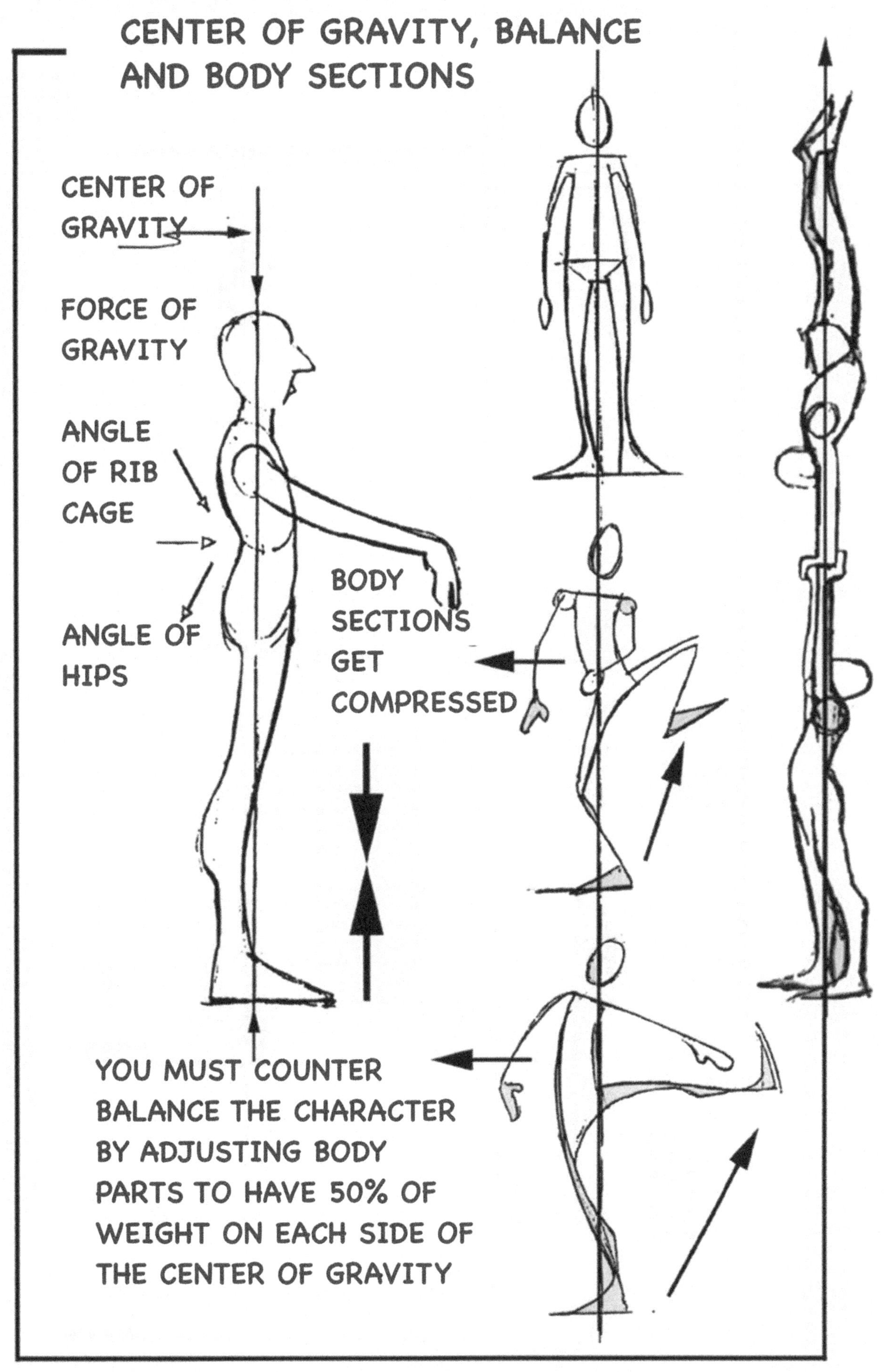

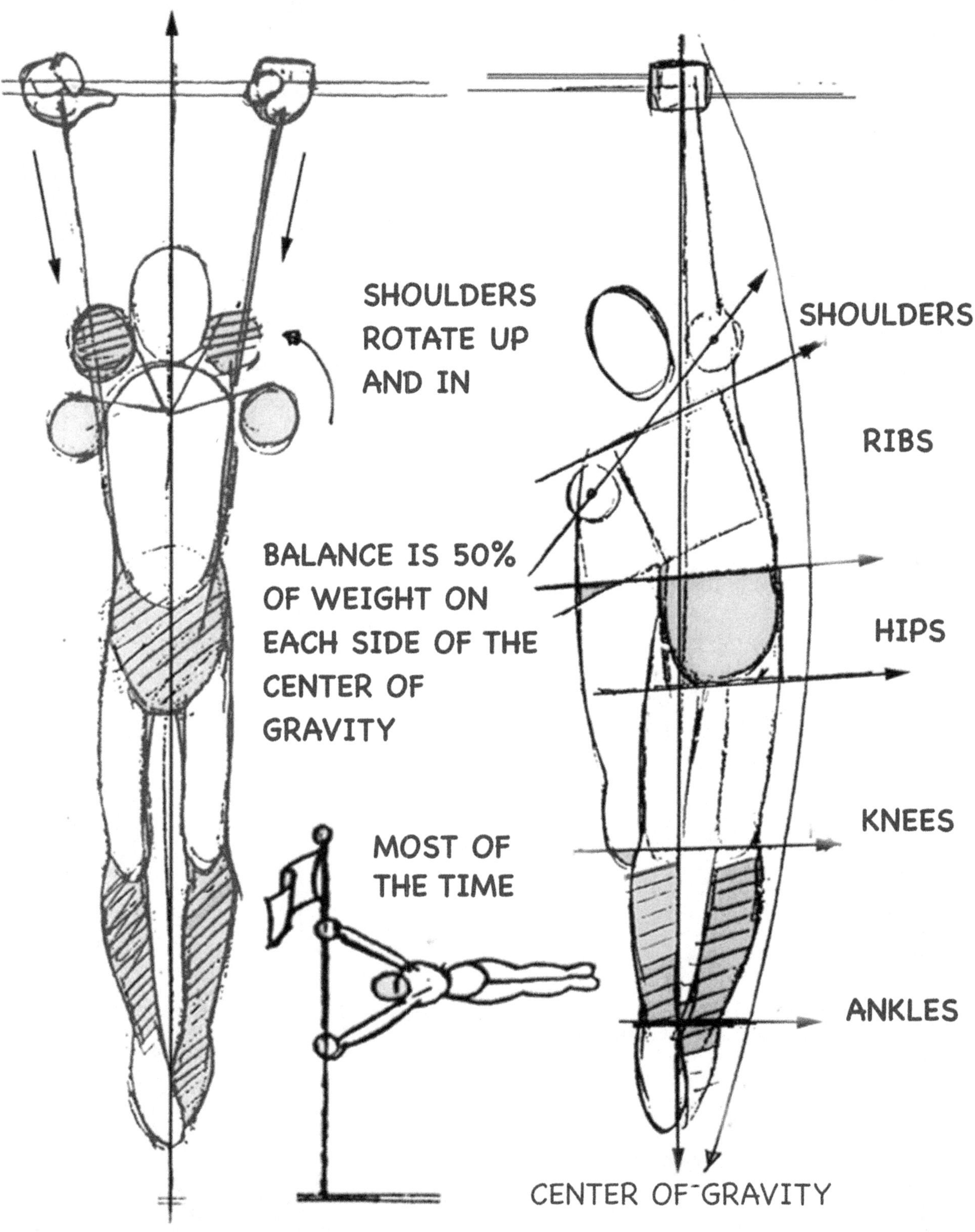

STUDY WHAT HAPPENS TO THE BODY WHILE UNDER DIFFERENT STRESSES, SUCH AS HANGING
SHOULDERS ROTATE UP AND IN
SHOULDERS
RIBS
BALANCE IS 50% OF WEIGHT ON EACH SIDE OF THE CENTER OF GRAVITY
HIPS
KNEES
MOST OF THE TIME
ANKLES
CENTER OF GRAVITY
PUT KNOWLEDGE TO WORK IN YOUR DRAWING, PLANNING AND ANIMATION

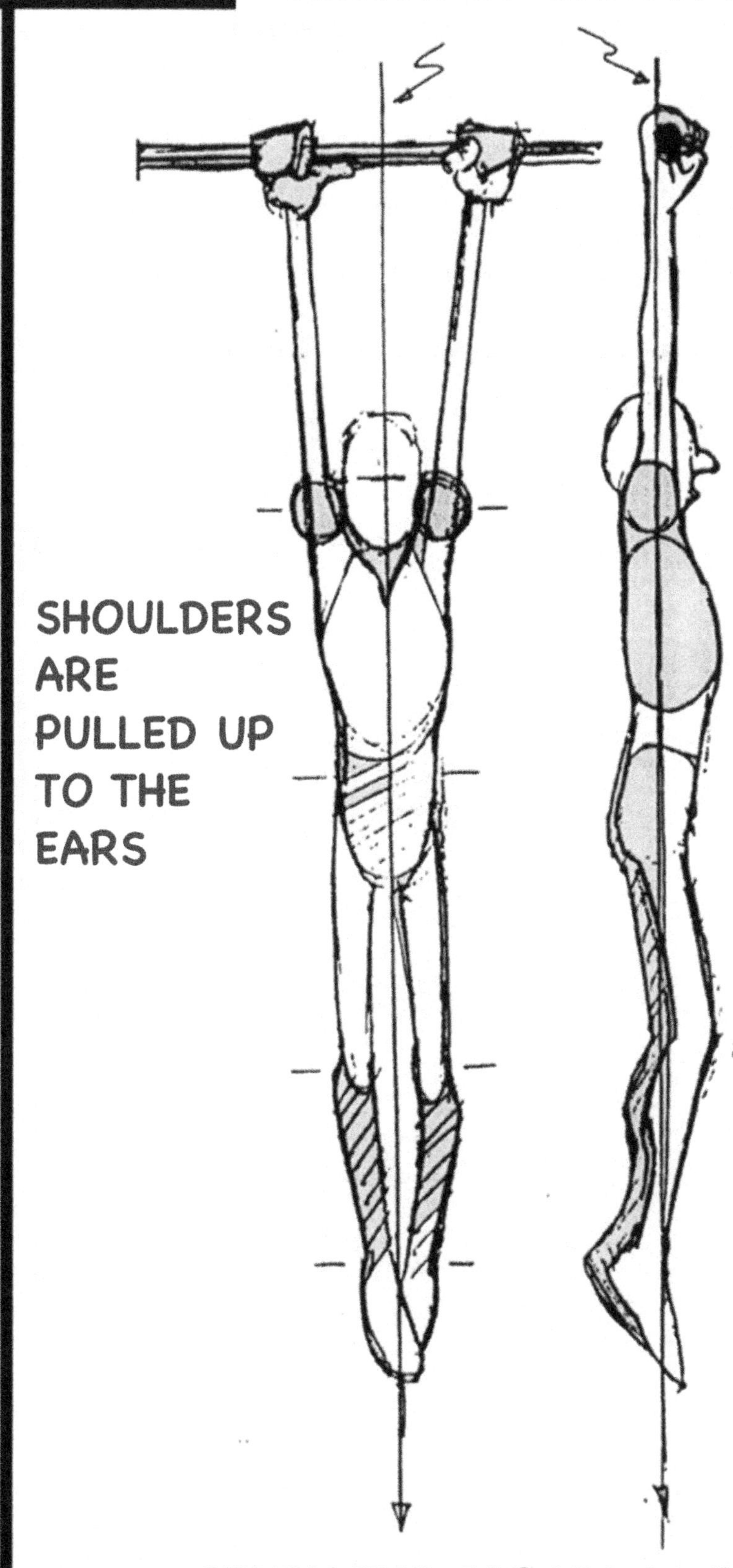

THE GREATEST
STRESS OF
WEIGHT IS ON
THE HANDS

SPINE CURVE

RELAXES AS

GRAVITY PULLS

DOWN INSTEAD

OF COMPRESSING

AS IT DOES

WHEN STANDING

HIPS, KNEES AND

ANKLES RELAX

STUDY THE FORCES AT PLAY IN
YOUR DRAWINGS AND ANIMATION

SIMPLIFIED ANATOMY

WITH KNOWLEDGE OF SUBJECT MATTER IT IS MUCH EASIER TO CREATE ROUGH BUT PRECISE THUMBNAIL SKETCHES

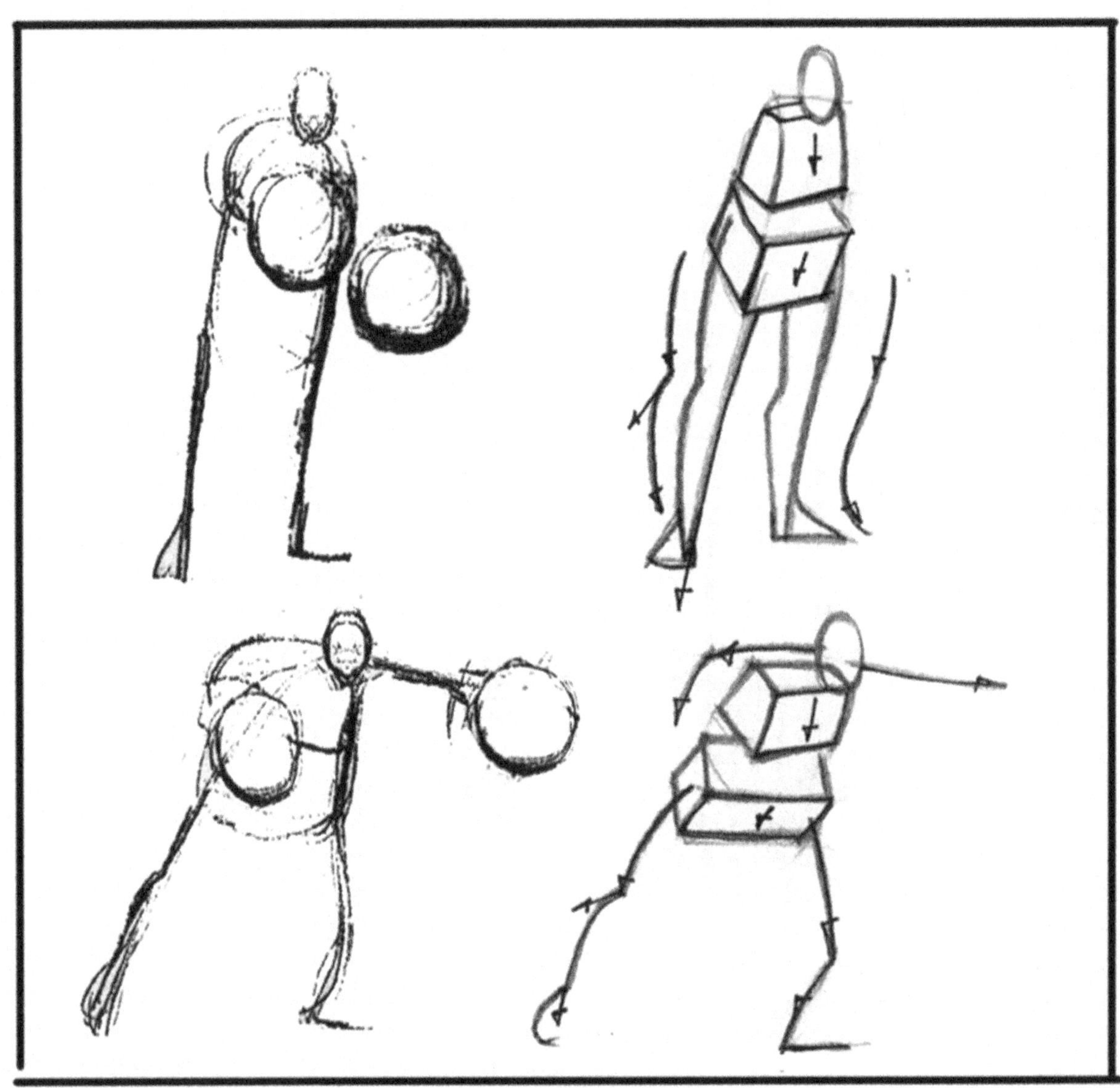

MAKE SURE TO LEARN THE FOUNDATION STRUCTURE OF ANYTHING THAT YOU ARE DRAWING. READ THE LISTED BOOKS TO STRENGTHEN YOUR KNOWLEDGE OF THE HUMAN BODY.

FIGURE DRAWING

WHEN YOU KNOW THE SIMPLE SHAPES AND ALIGNMENT OF THE BODY'S SECTIONS, YOU CAN EXPLORE STYLES WITH CONFIDENCE.

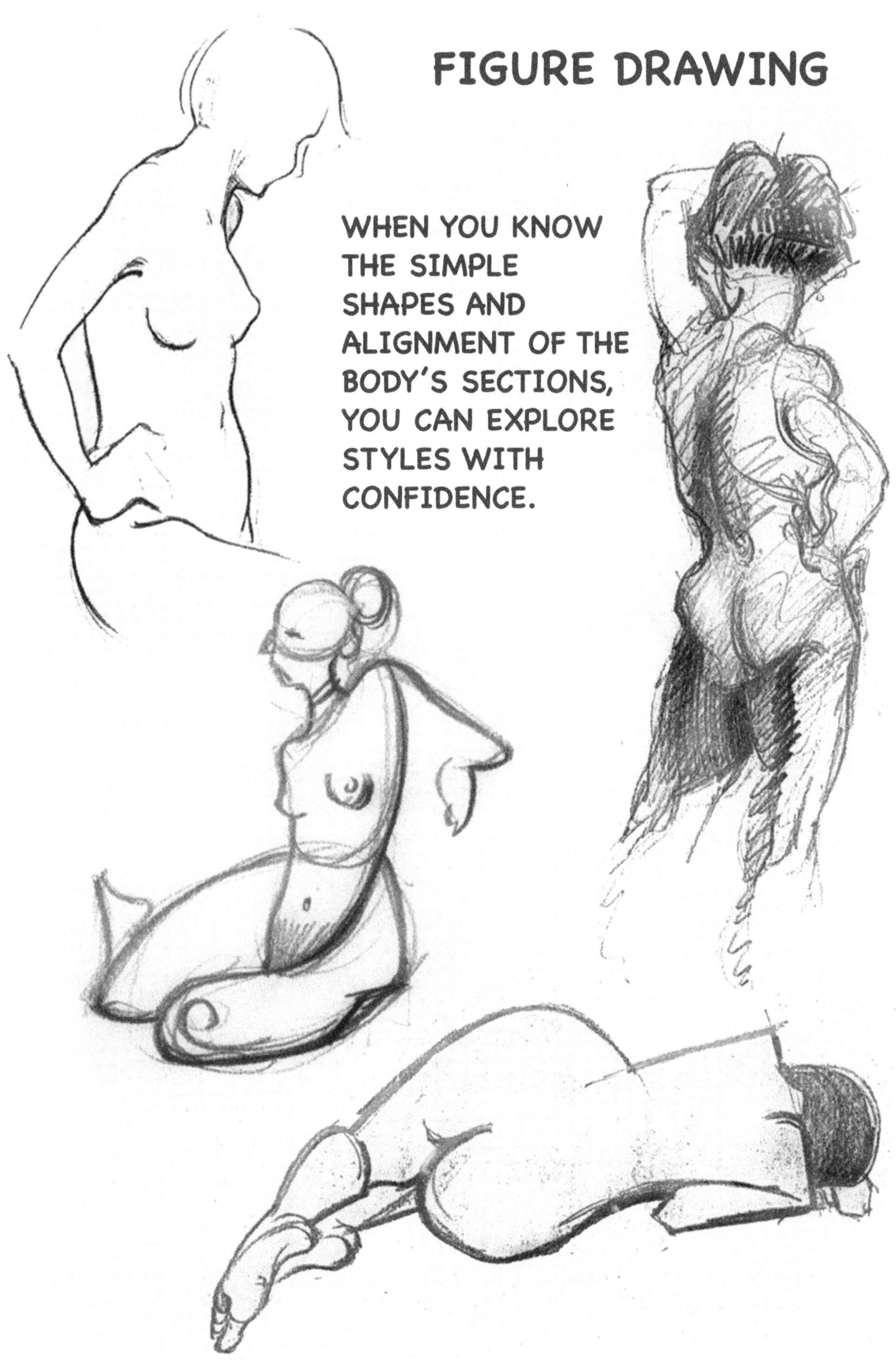

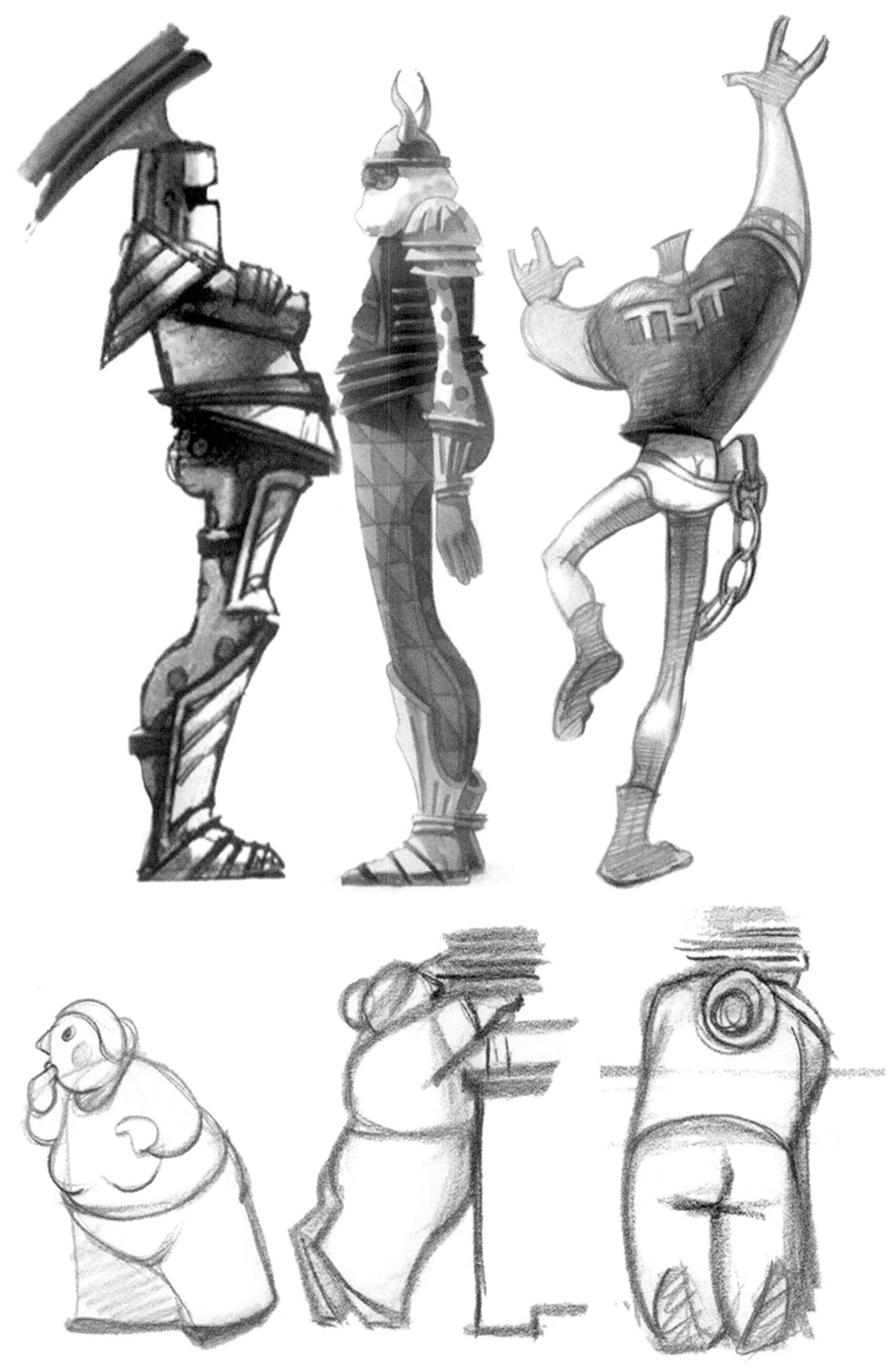

TNT

WARM-UPS

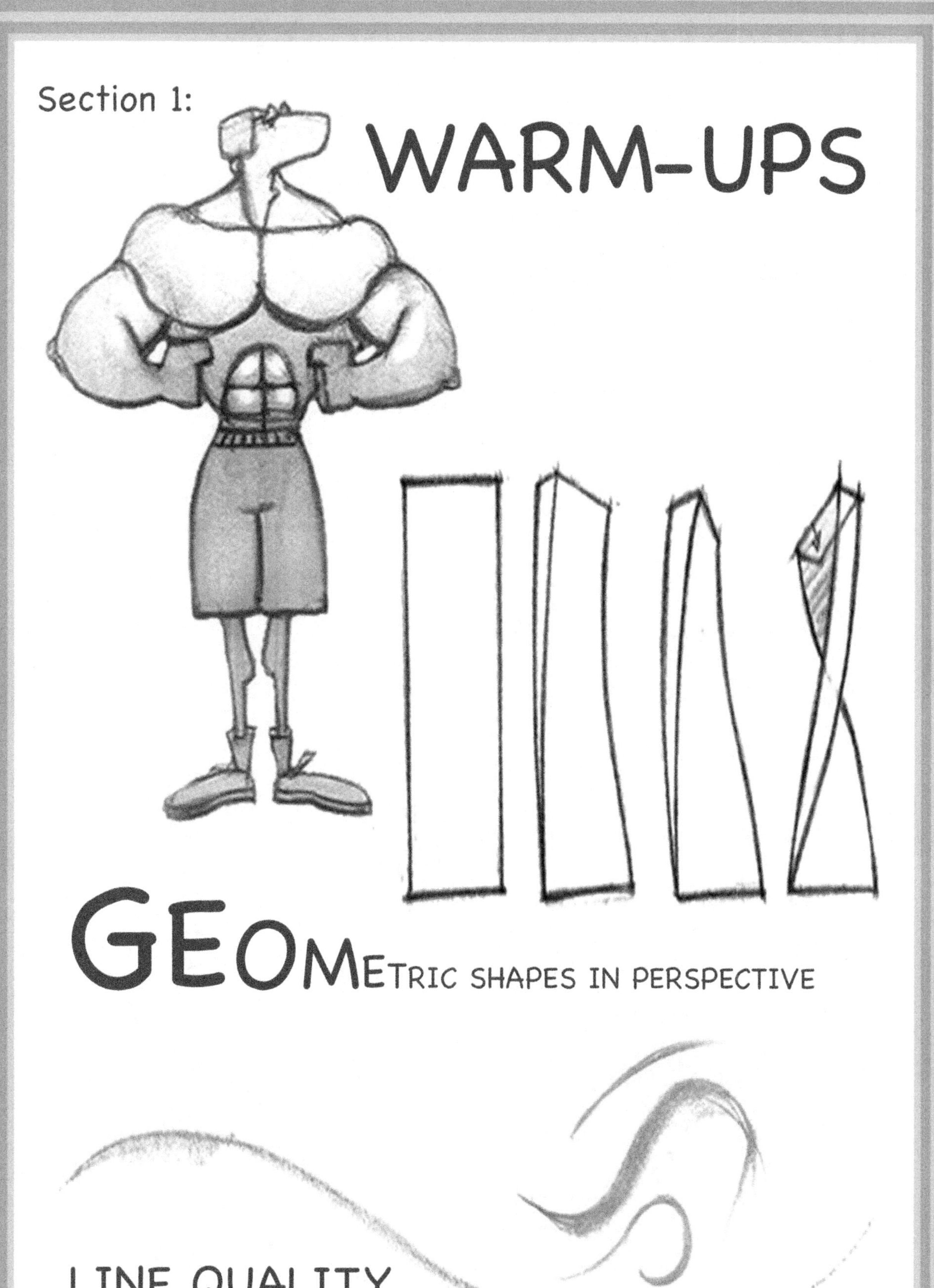

GEOMETRIC SHAPES IN PERSPECTIVE

LINE QUALITY

LINE VARIATION AND QUALITY

Line variation can greatly enhance your drawings when used intentionally. Line variation helps to explain specific qualities such as force, compression and light direction.

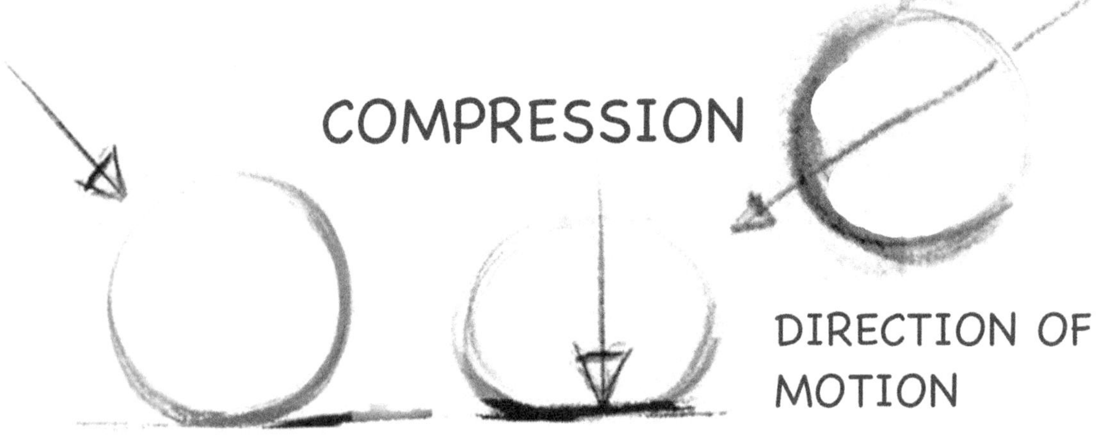

LIGHT DIRECTION

Use a lighter line on the side of the object that is getting direct light and a darker line to represent the shaded side.

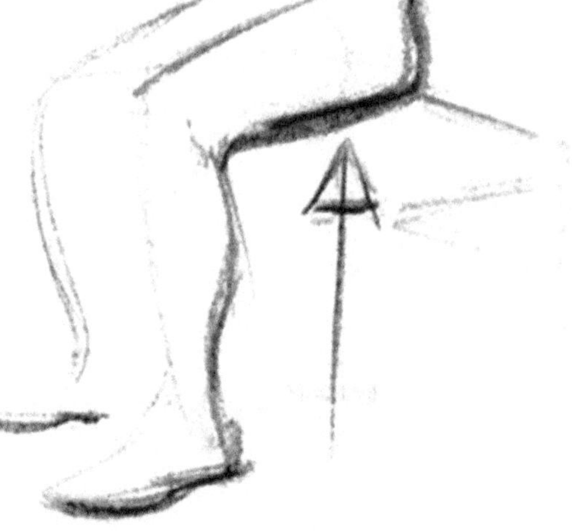

LINE VARIATION

Line's thickness, direction and shape present psychological implications to the viewer. A sense of motion, strength, weight, even emotion are all implied when proper line quality is used.

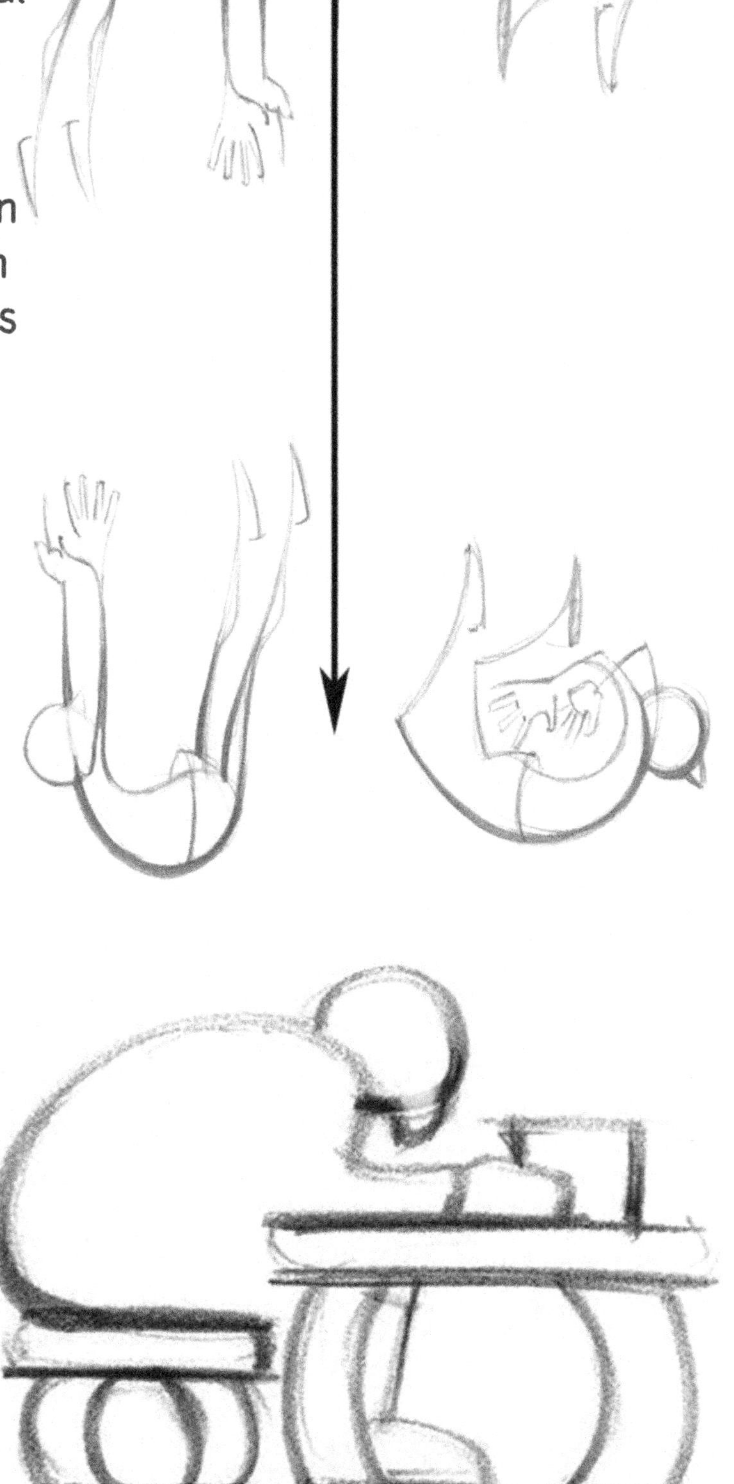

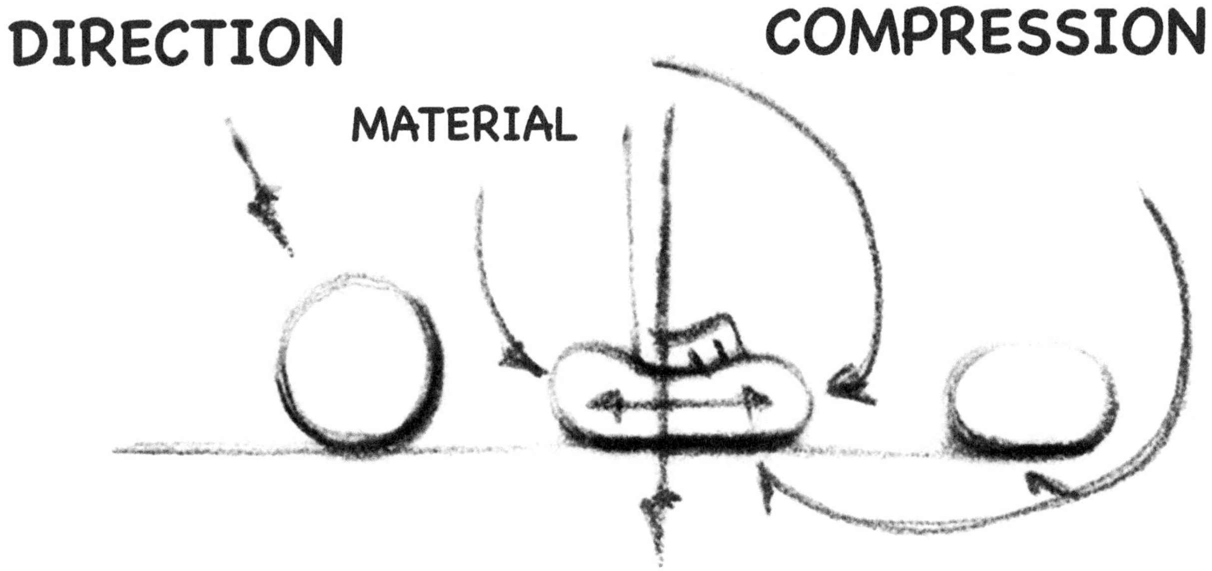

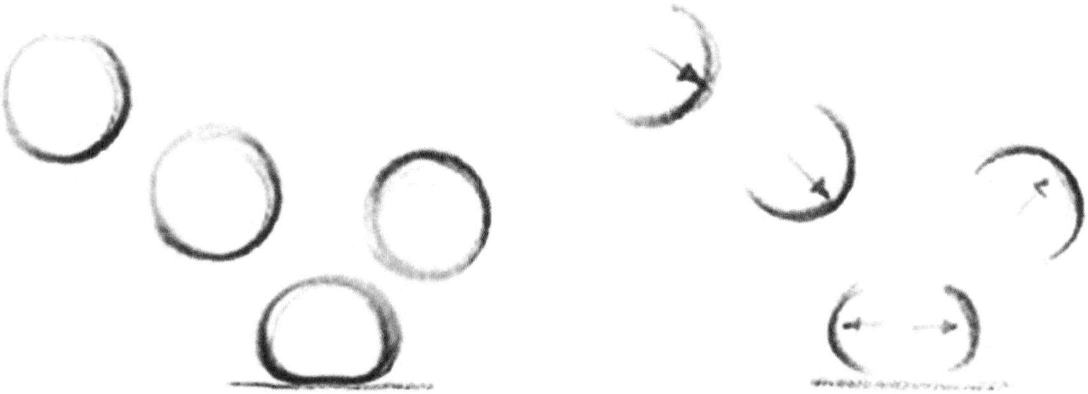

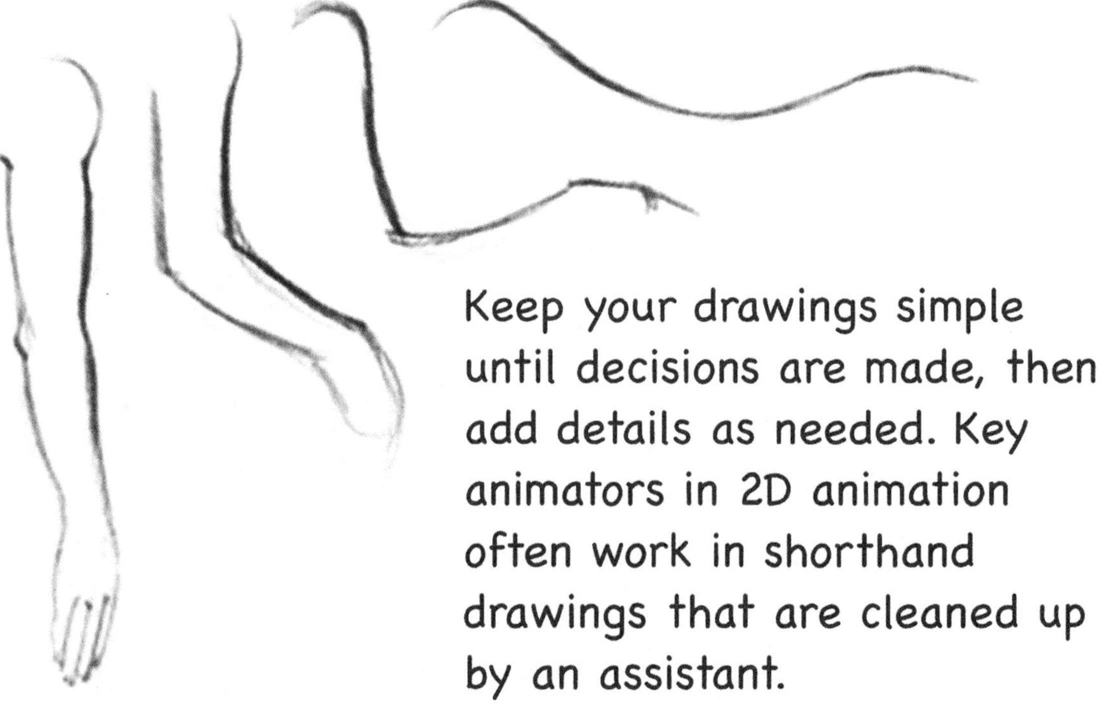

DIRECTION

MATERIAL

COMPRESSION

Use line variation in planning and animation to imply motion.

Keep your drawings simple until decisions are made, then add details as needed. Key animators in 2D animation often work in shorthand drawings that are cleaned up by an assistant.

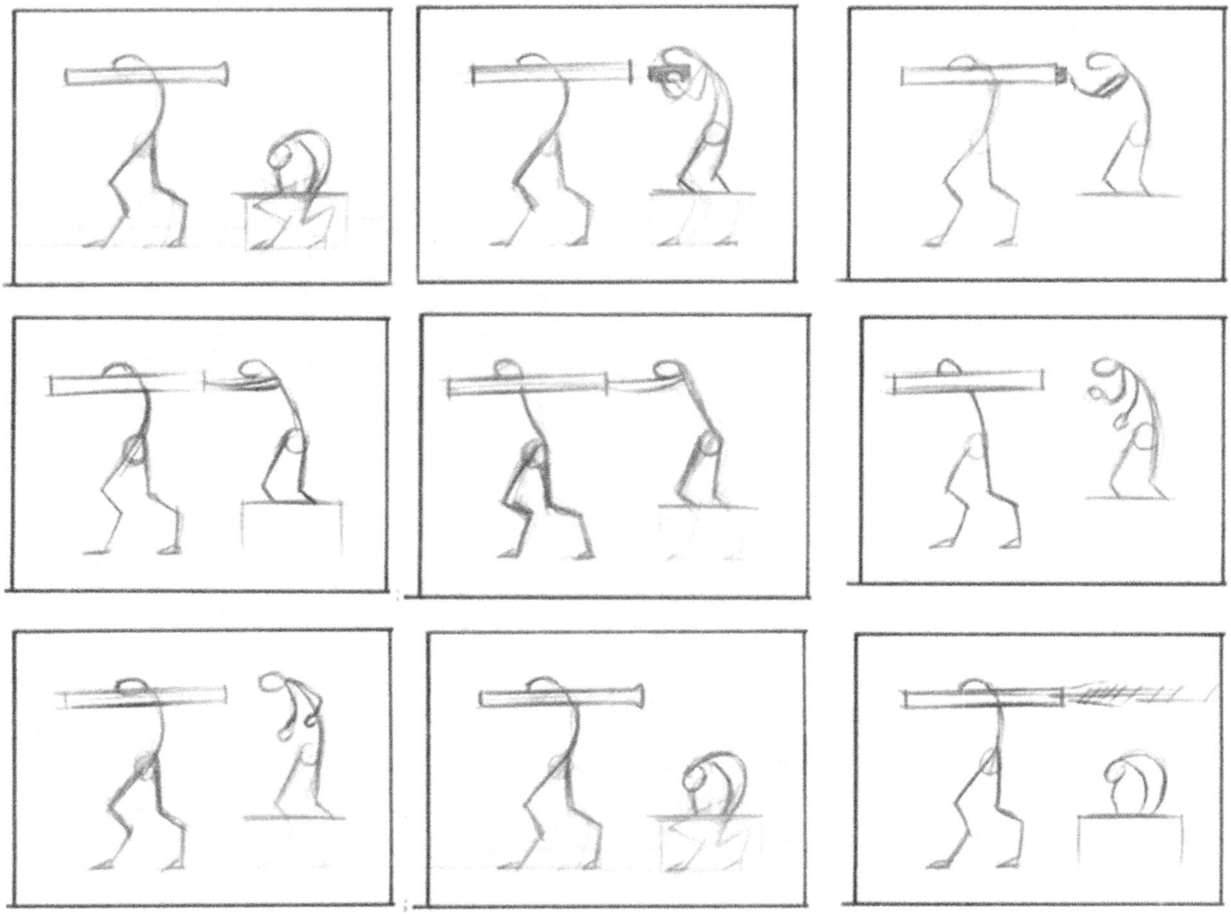

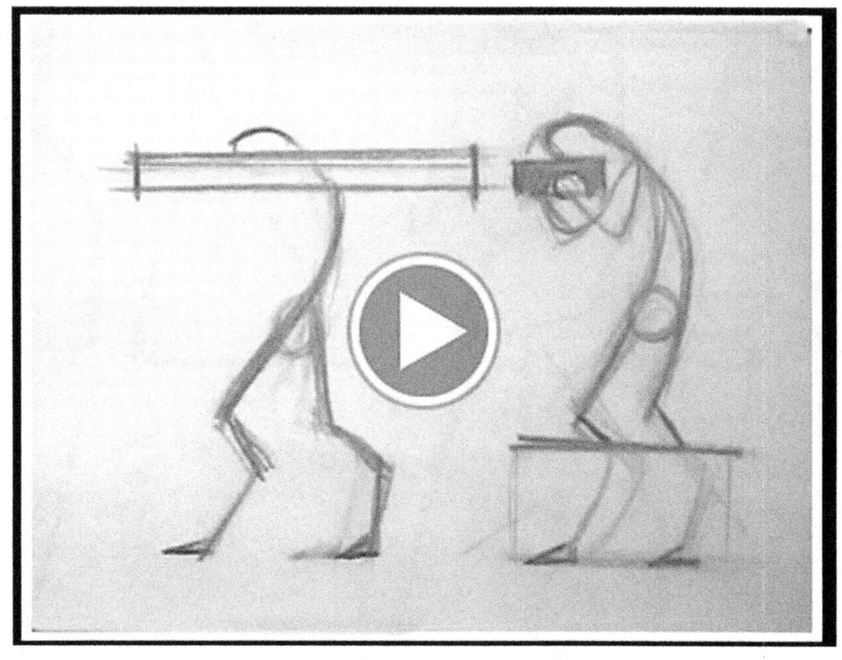

2 simple tests for MIB II in pre-production at ILM

Movie files can be seen at www.anamie.com

GEOMETRIC SHAPES

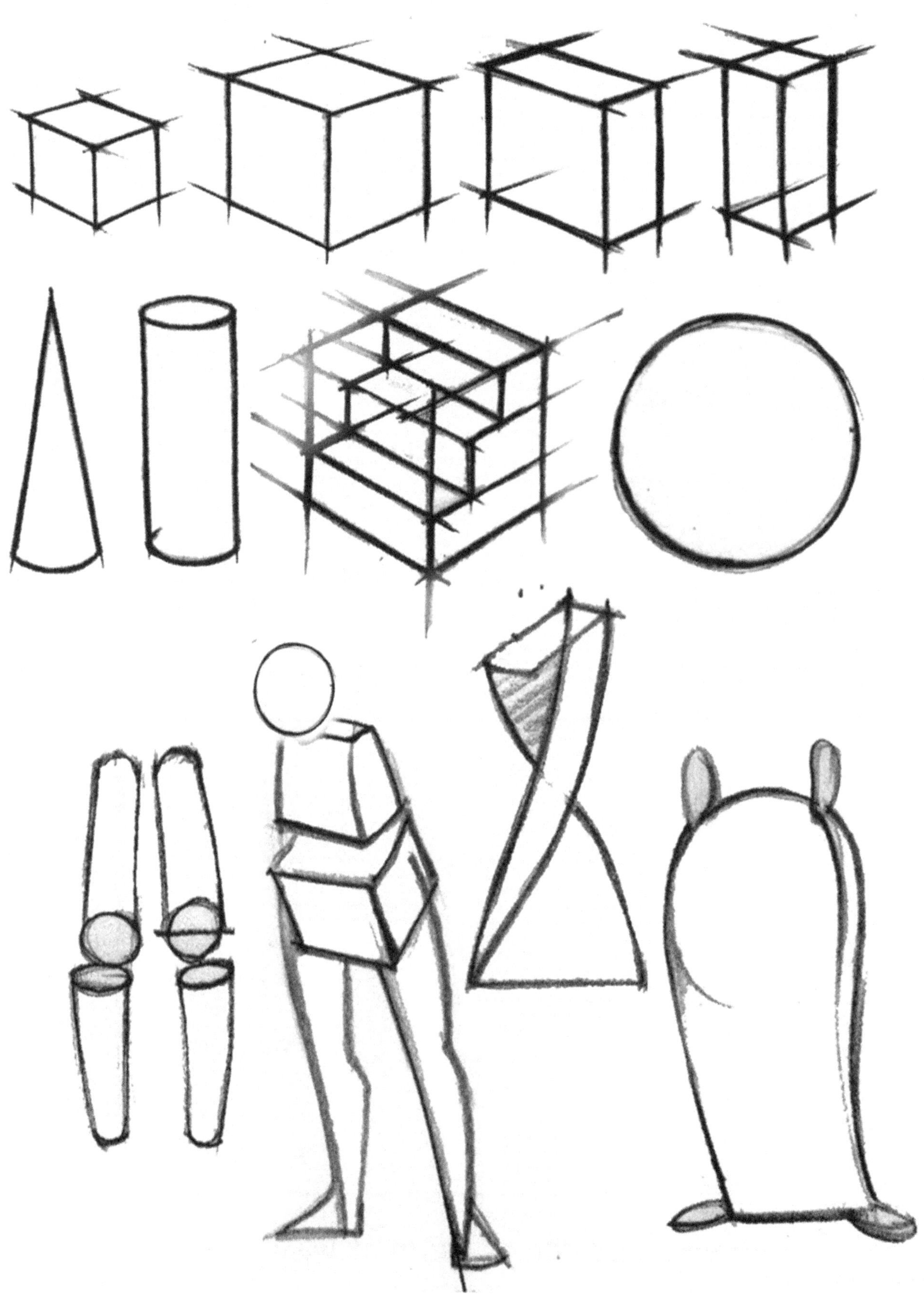

It is essential that you know simplified body structure and how the body parts work when connected as a unit.

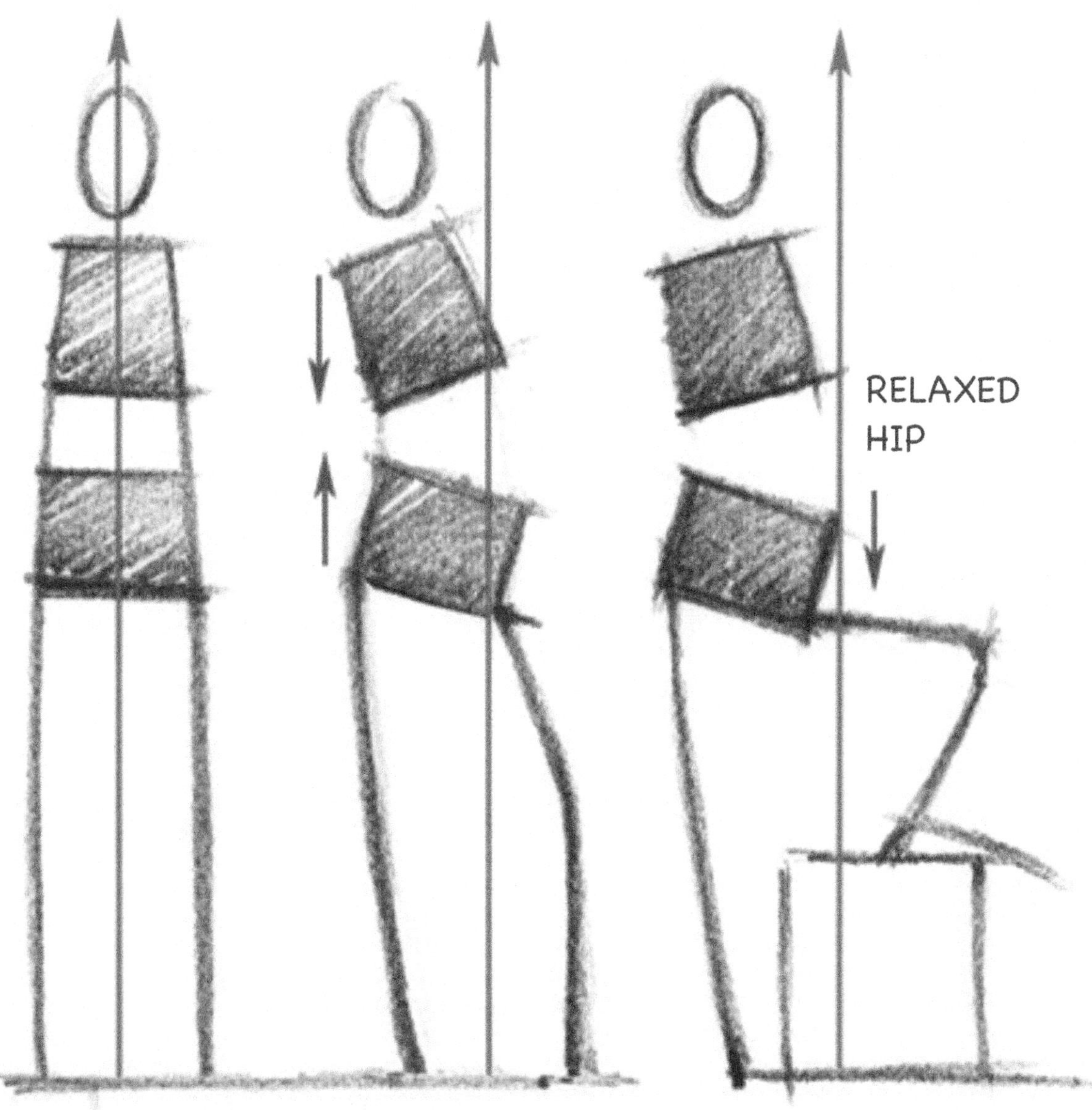

When at rest and balanced, the rib cage and hips are level.

When there is more weight on one side, the hip on that side is driven up and the shoulder drops.

Even if a foot is raised and resting on a box, the hip not supporting the weight is usually relaxed and down.

Learn the **simplified sections of the body** and their alignment - pages 49-61. The spine unites the body and naturally adjusts to help us maintain balance.

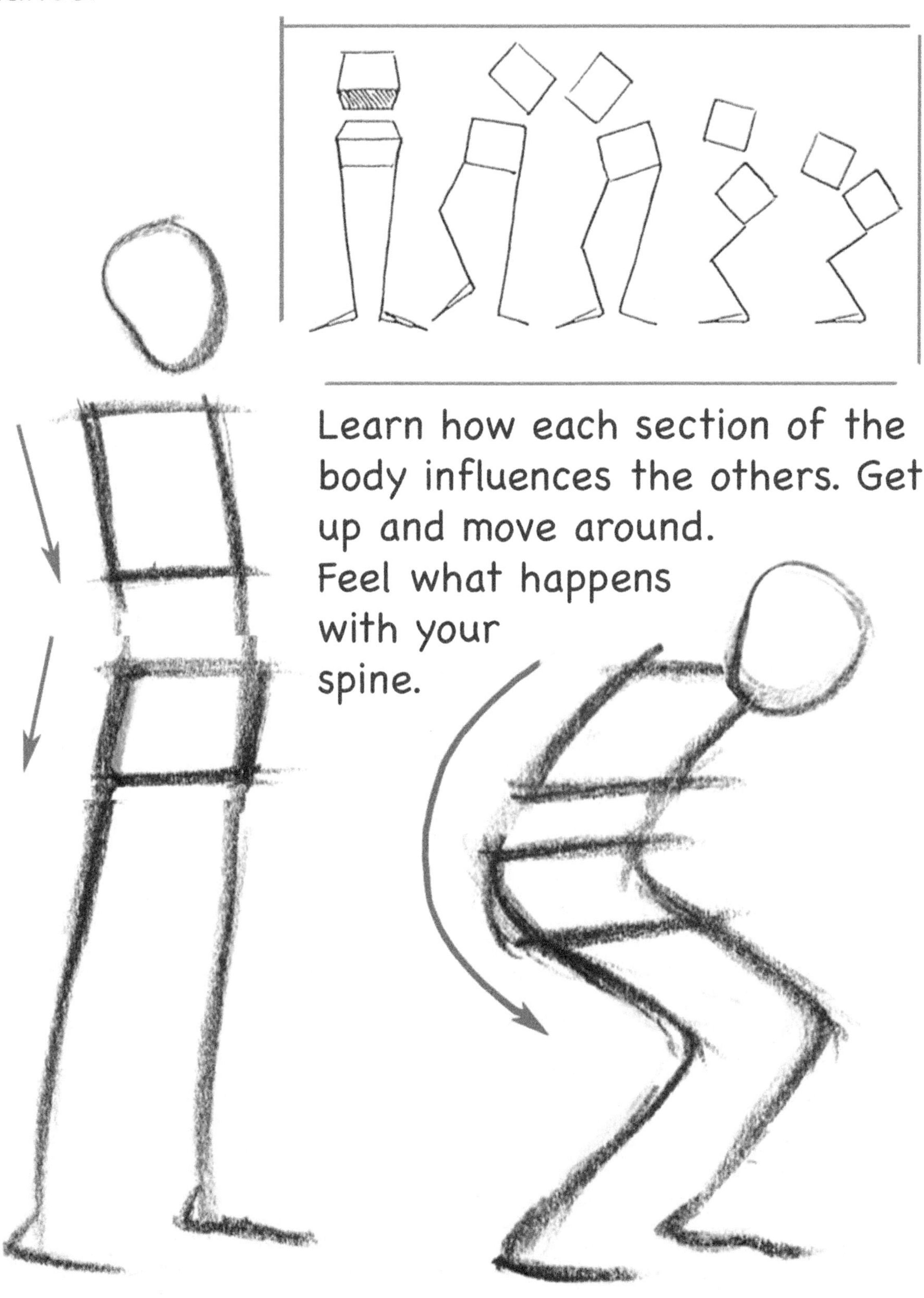

Learn how each section of the body influences the others. Get up and move around. Feel what happens with your spine.

Draw cubes, boxes, blocks, spheres, cones and tubes. Go to the library and get Basic Principles of Design by Manfred Maier and study Volume One. Practice keeping lines parallel – don't make them converge in forced perspective.

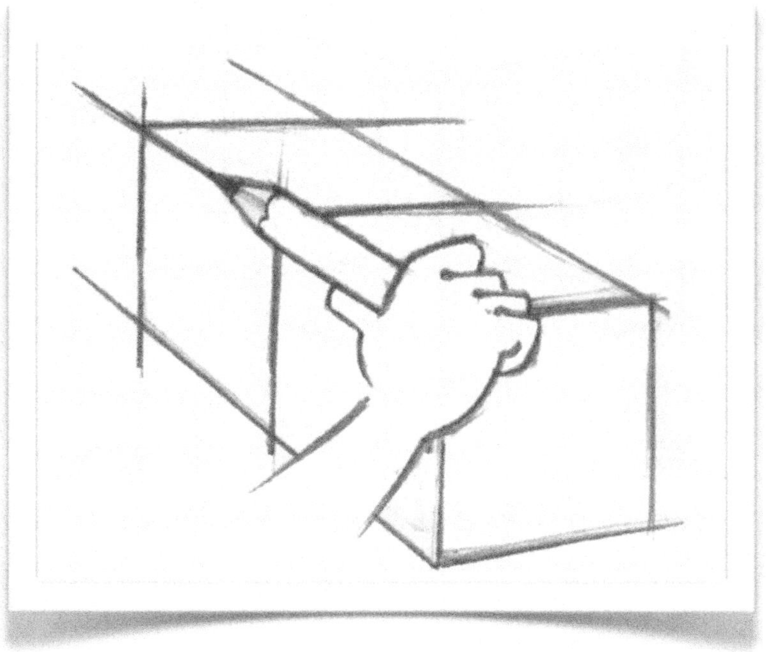

Draw light construction lines that go beyond the edges of what you are sketching. This allows you keep the lines parallel or converging slightly. The light lines create a see through version of the object; an under drawing showing the edges that are not visible. It is a wireframe construction that you can build on. Use a soft pencil – 4B or 6B.

Take your time; be precise with the lines. Start light and darken the lines that represent the exterior edges you want to see.

Use diagonals to locate the center of the shape. This allows you to find the perspective center which shows the shape's diminishing proportions as it goes away. Draw lines from corner to corner – where they cross is the center of the object.

GEOMETRIC SHAPES

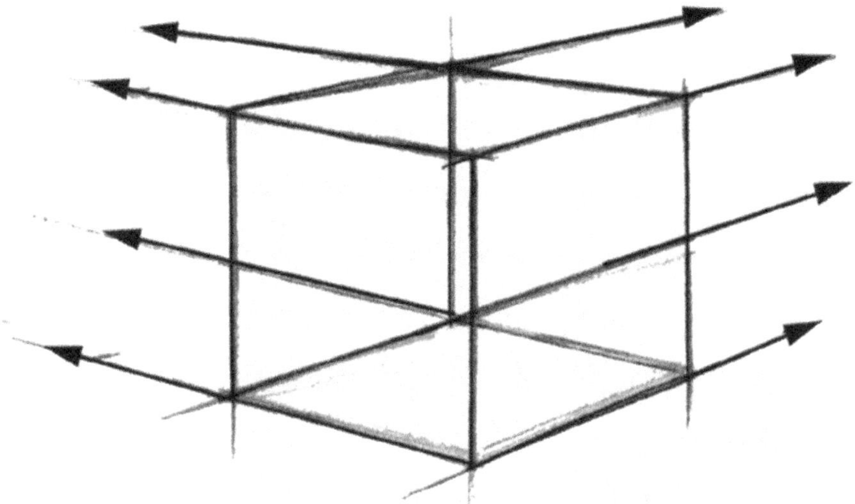

Draw the ground plane first and build up from there. Remember to make all perspective construction lines parallel or slightly converging.

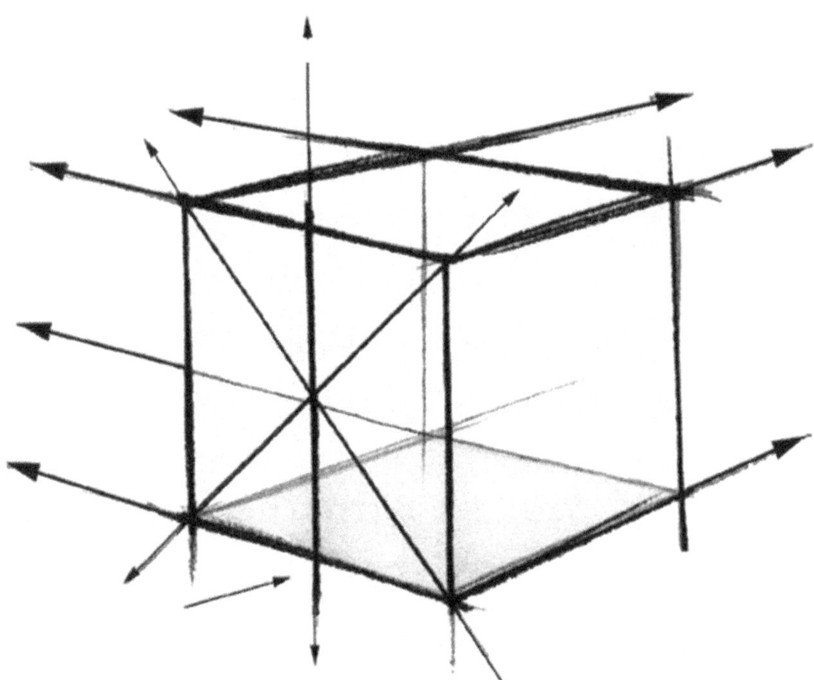

Learn the principles of perspective but don't restrict yourself to rulers and vanishing points. Draw free hand and train yourself to make straight lines parallel to one another.

DISSECTING CUBES

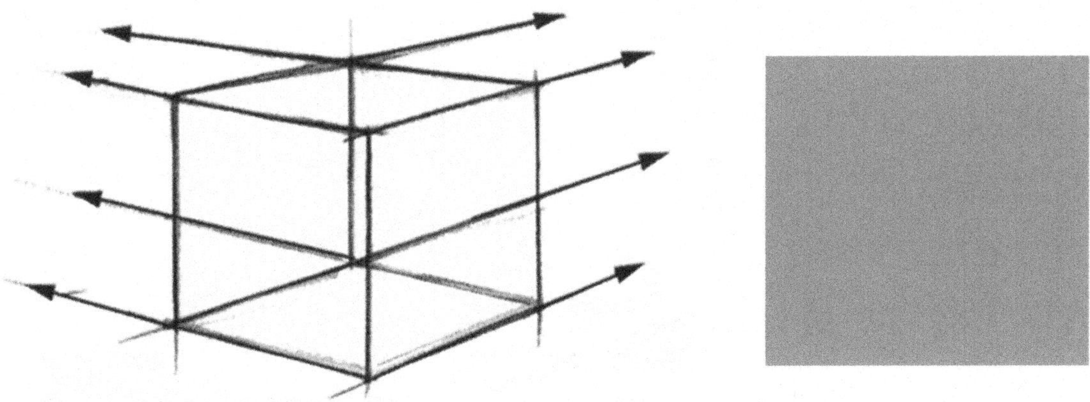

Start to understand geometric shapes by dissecting cubes into smaller shapes.

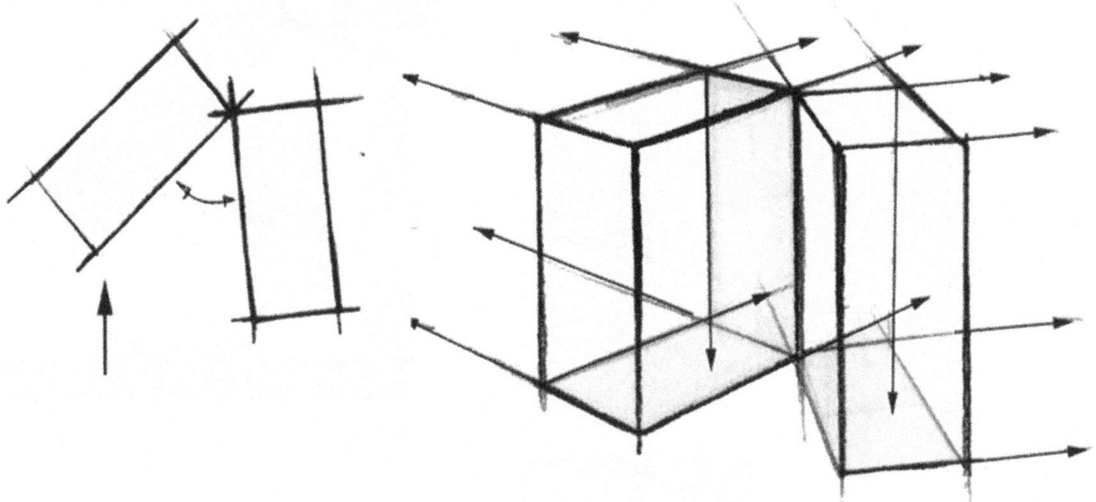

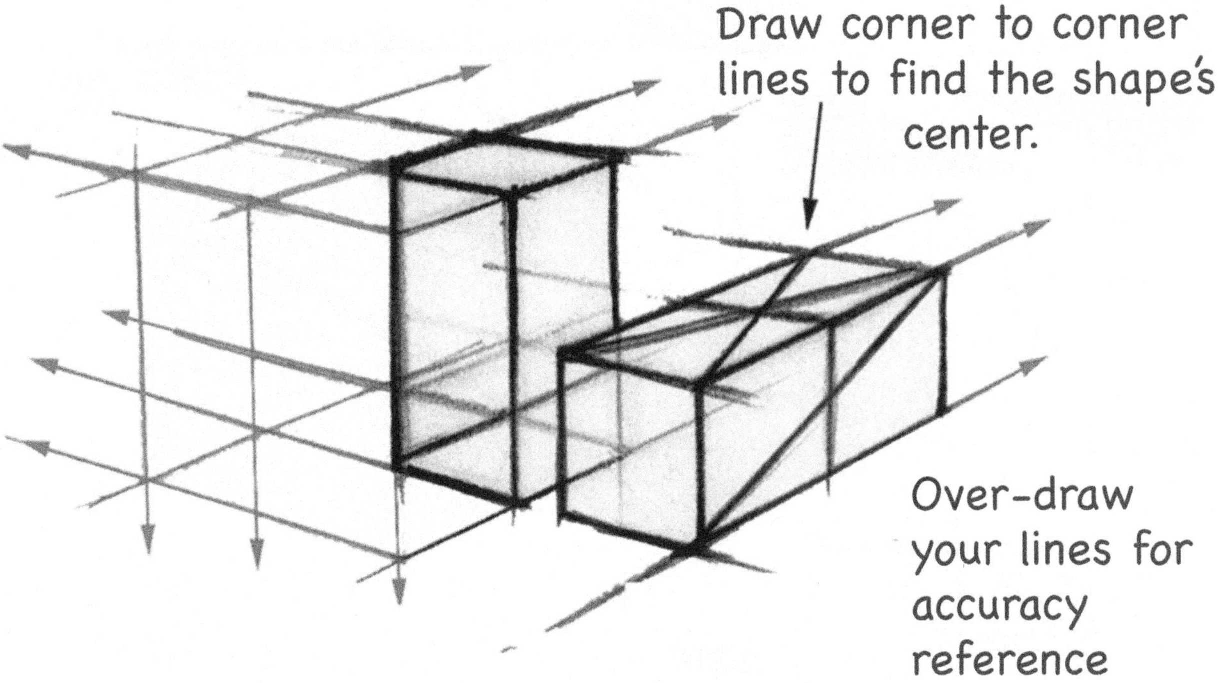

Draw corner to corner lines to find the shape's center.

Over-draw your lines for accuracy reference

GEOMETRIC SHAPES

Think of this exercise as cutting and removing sections of a cube.

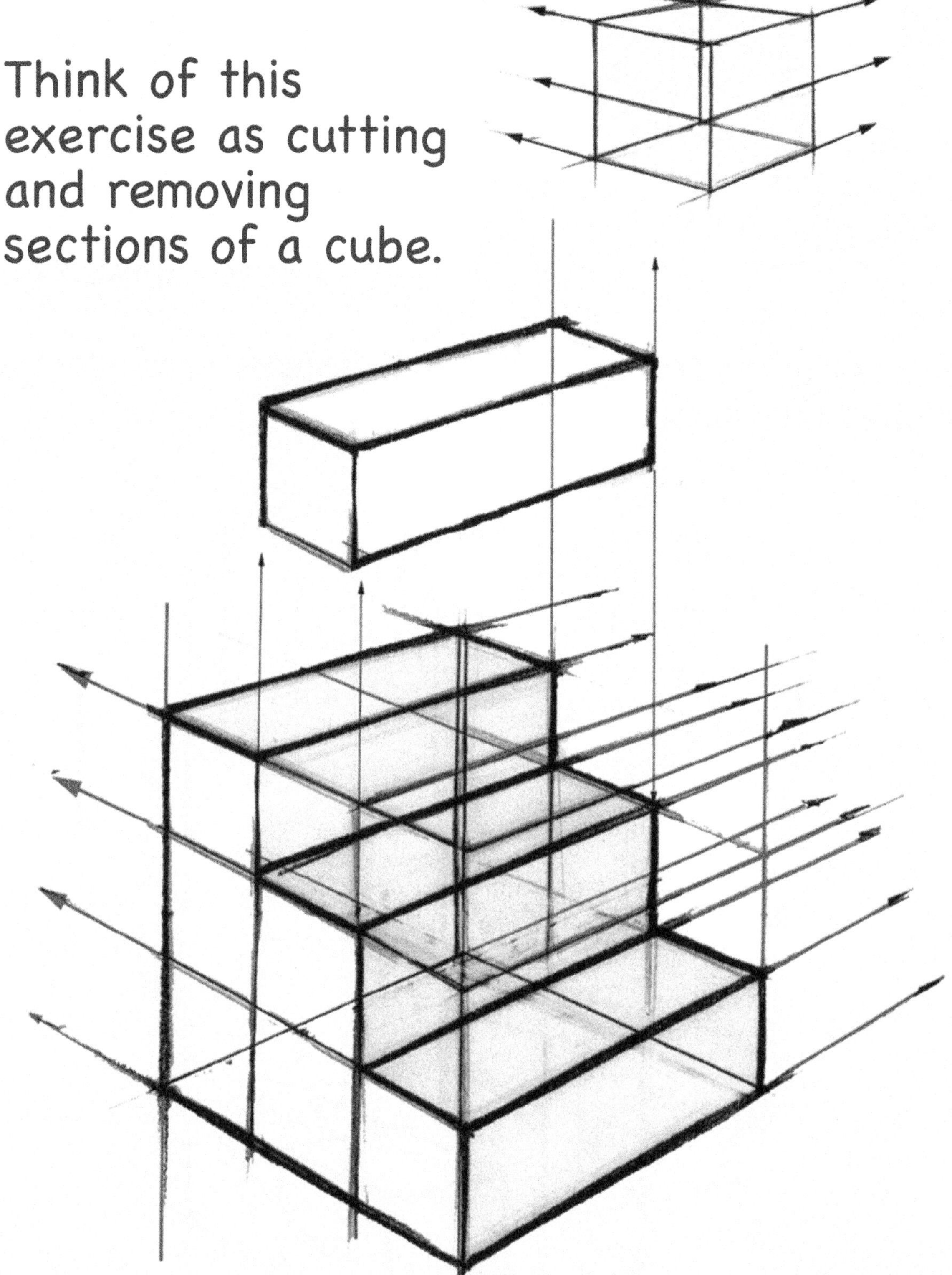

Draw the back of the object with see-through structural lines. Know the form.

SIMPLIFIED ELLIPSE

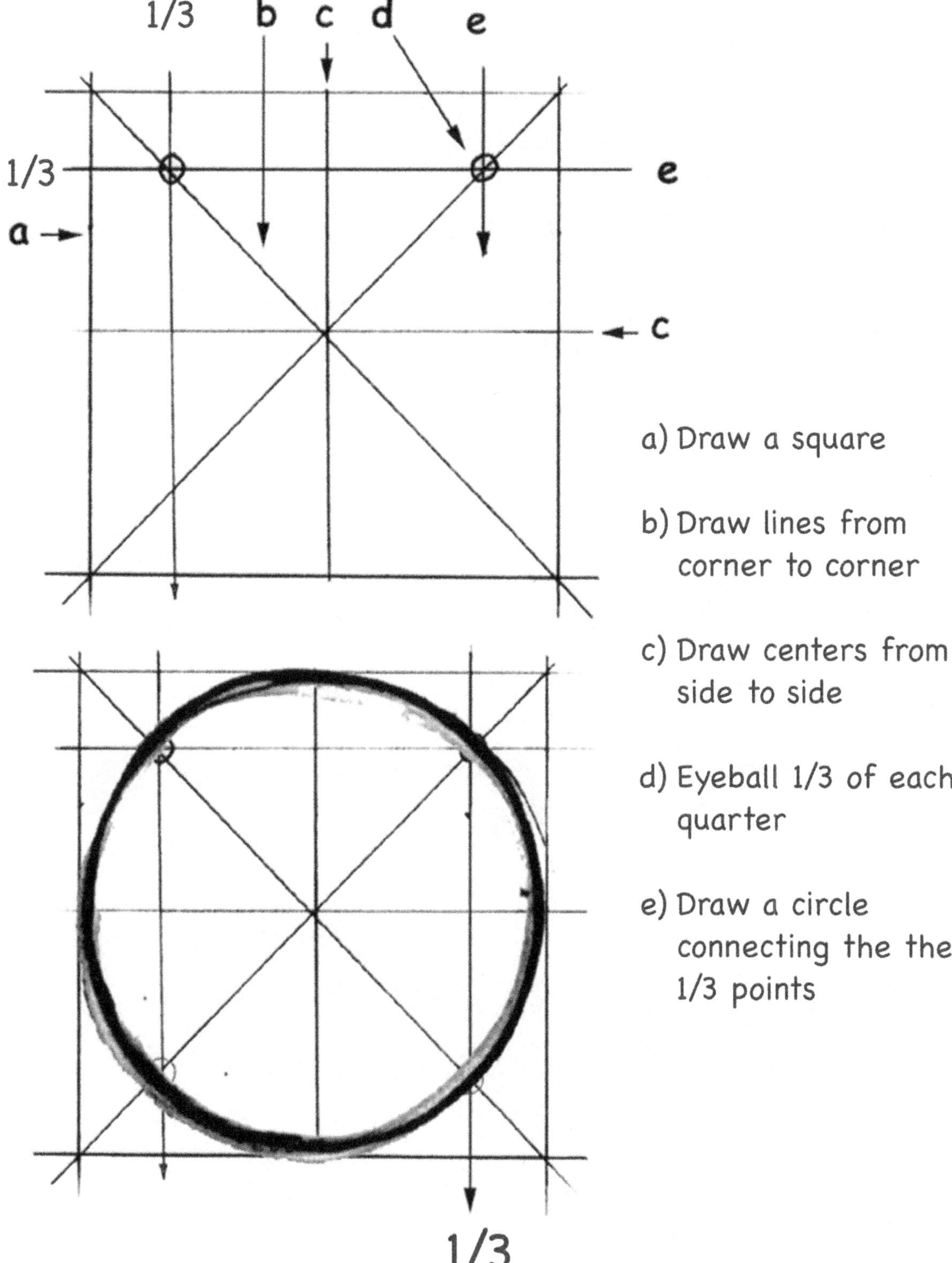

a) Draw a square

b) Draw lines from corner to corner

c) Draw centers from side to side

d) Eyeball 1/3 of each quarter

e) Draw a circle connecting the the 1/3 points

Draw a circle connecting the 1/3 points

a) Draw squares in **perspective**
b) Draw corner diagonals
c) Draw centers
d) Eyeball 1/3 of each quarter
e) Draw an ellipse connecting
   the 1/3 points

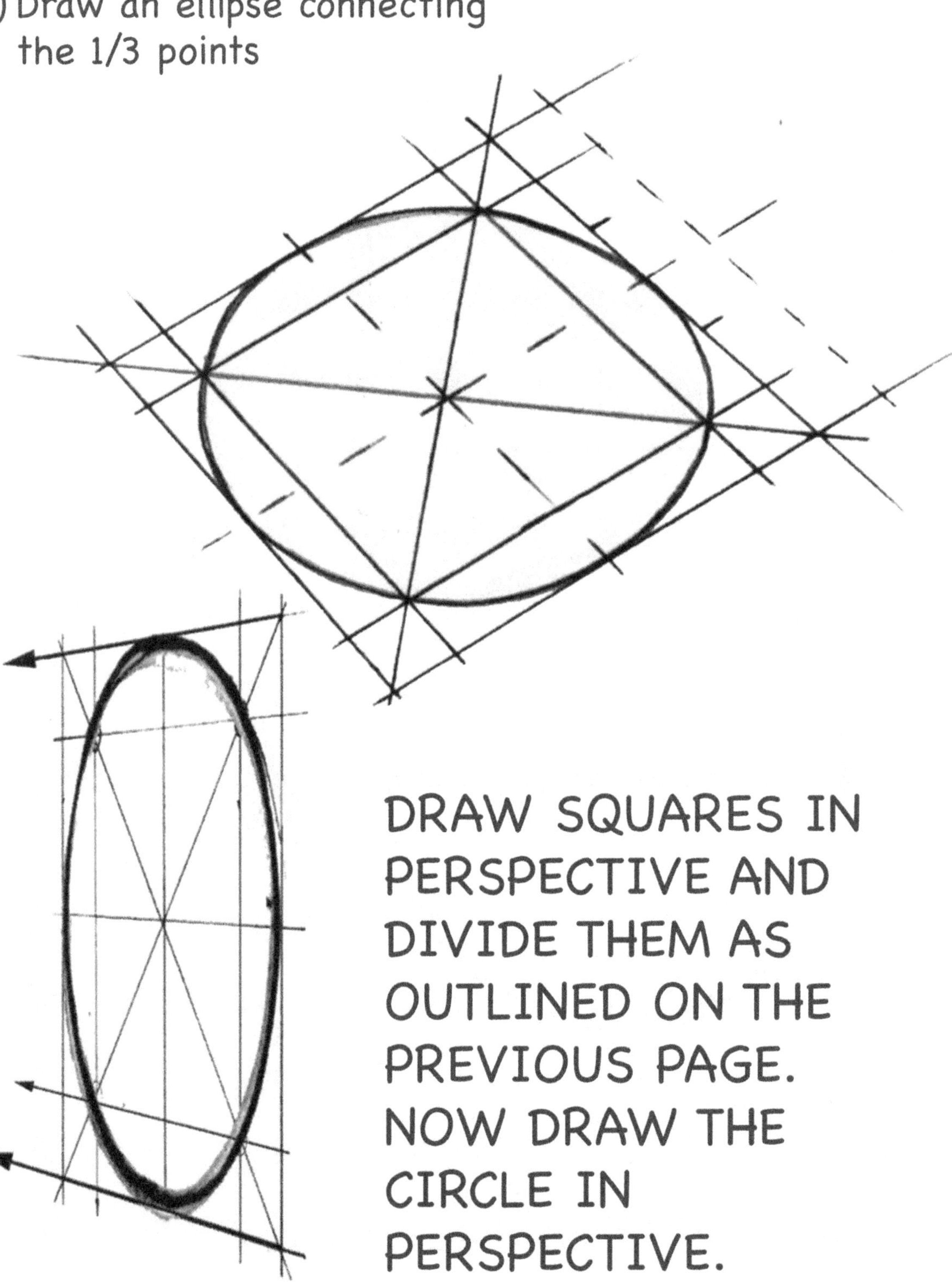

DRAW SQUARES IN
PERSPECTIVE AND
DIVIDE THEM AS
OUTLINED ON THE
PREVIOUS PAGE.
NOW DRAW THE
CIRCLE IN
PERSPECTIVE.

ELLIPSES and CYLINDERS

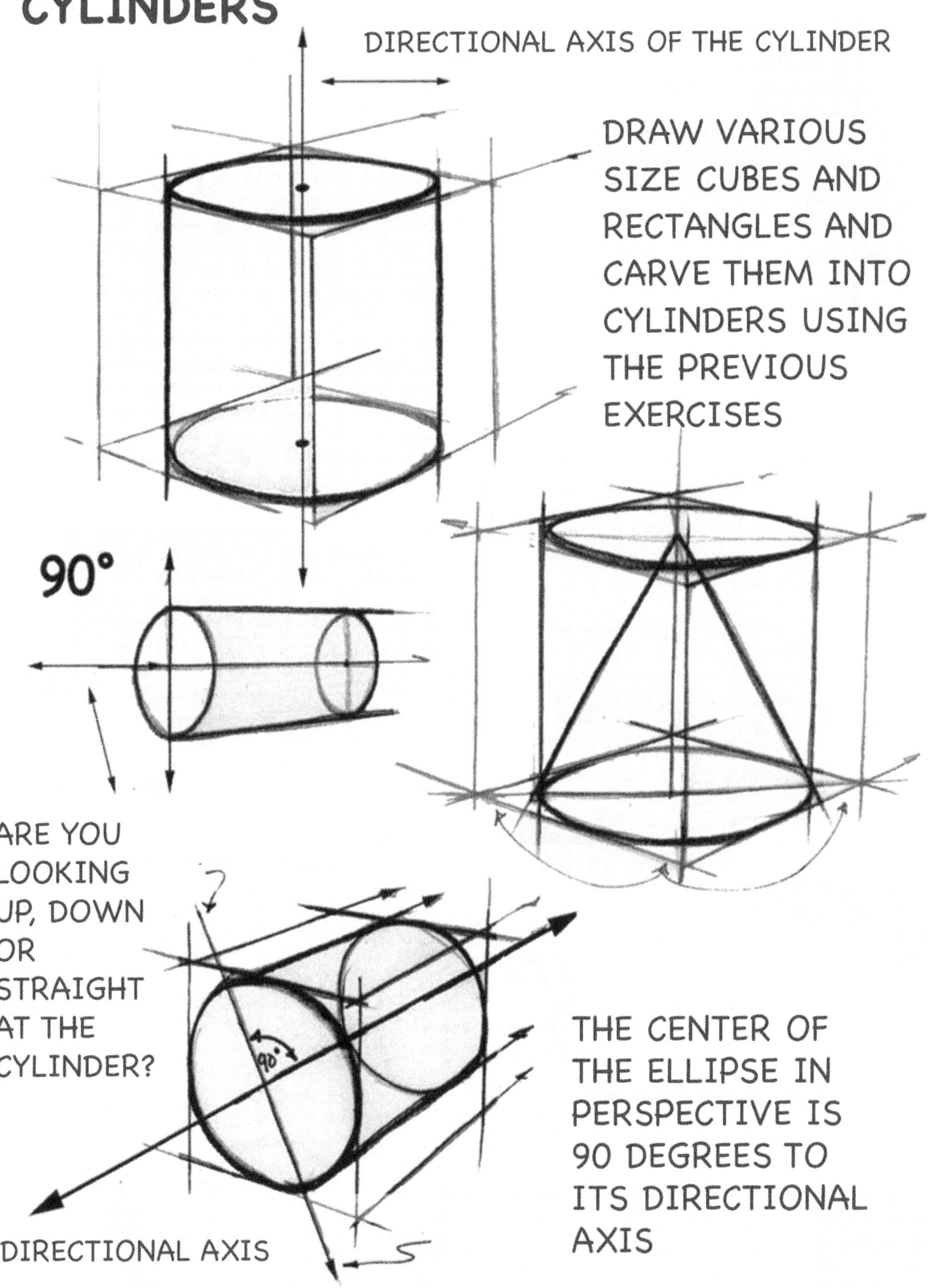

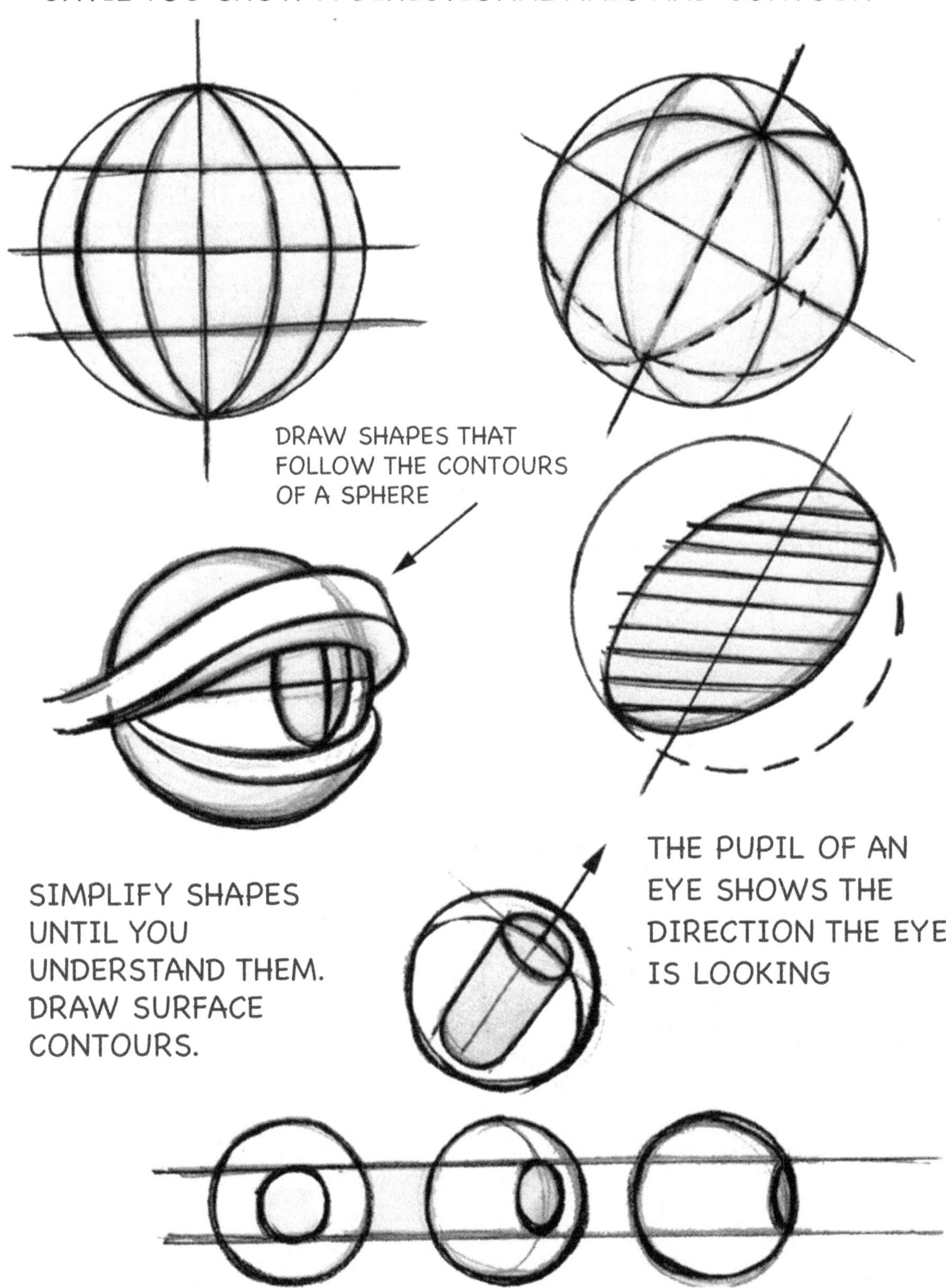

SPHERE

A SPHERE (CIRCLE) LOOKS THE SAME FROM ALL ANGLES
UNTIL YOU SHOW A DIRECTIONAL AXIS AND CONTOUR

WARM-UPS

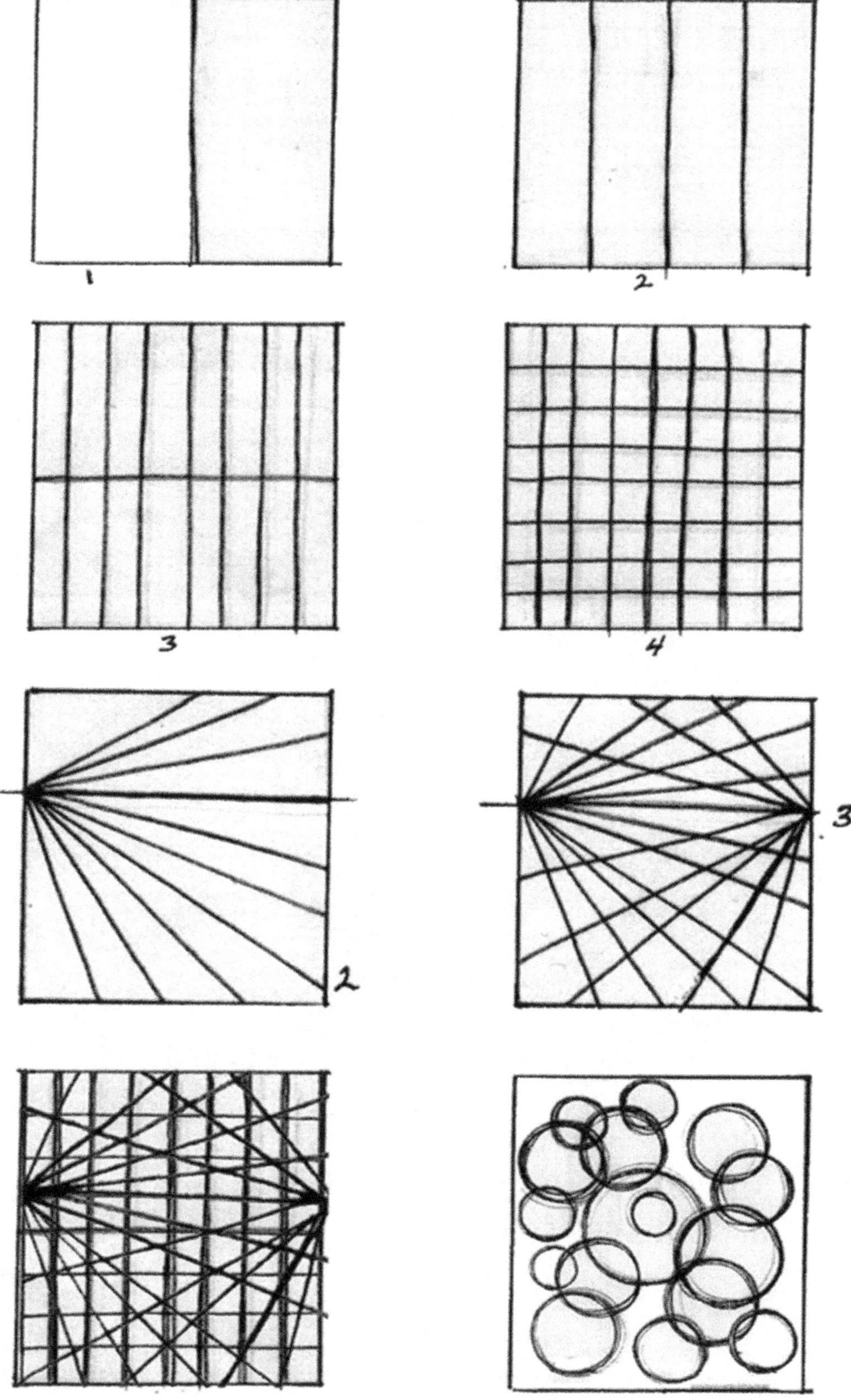

CIRCLE WARM-UPS

AS WITH ANY EXERCISE, MUSCLES SHOULD BE LOOSENED UP FIRST. USE YOUR ENTIRE ARM, NOT JUST THE WRIST, DRAW FROM YOUR SHOULDER. COVER A PAGE WITH VARIOUS SIZE CIRCLES AND DRAW IN BOTH DIRECTIONS. DRAW THICK AND THIN, DARK AND LIGHT LINES. DO NOT WORRY ABOUT WHAT THE PAGE LOOKS LIKE - OVERLAP THE CIRCLES.

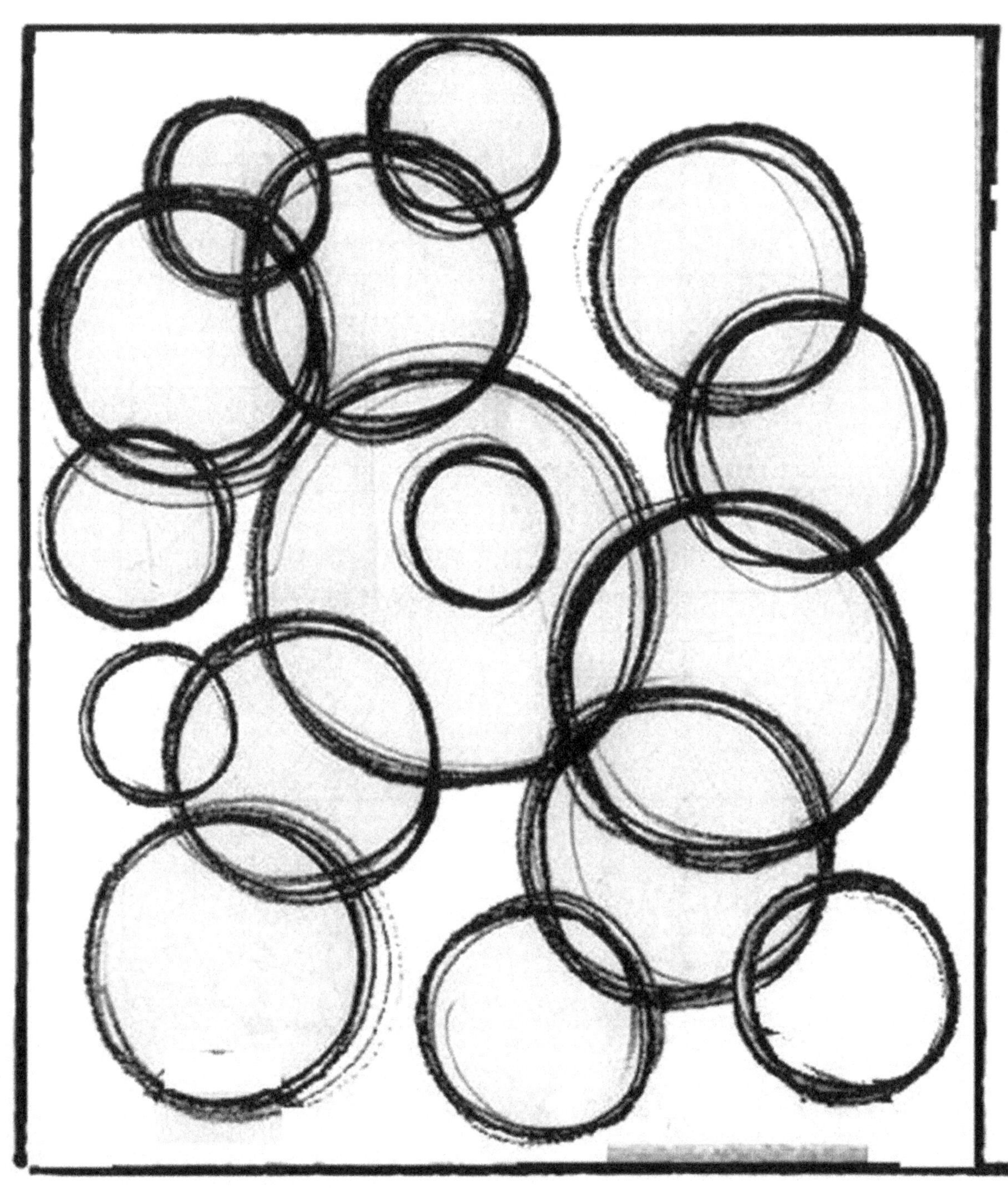

STRAIGHT LINE WARM-UPS:

Draw from your shoulder. Don't rotate the paper.
a) Divide the page in half vertically
b) Divide the halves in half
c) Continue a third and fourth division
d) Do the same with horizontal lines

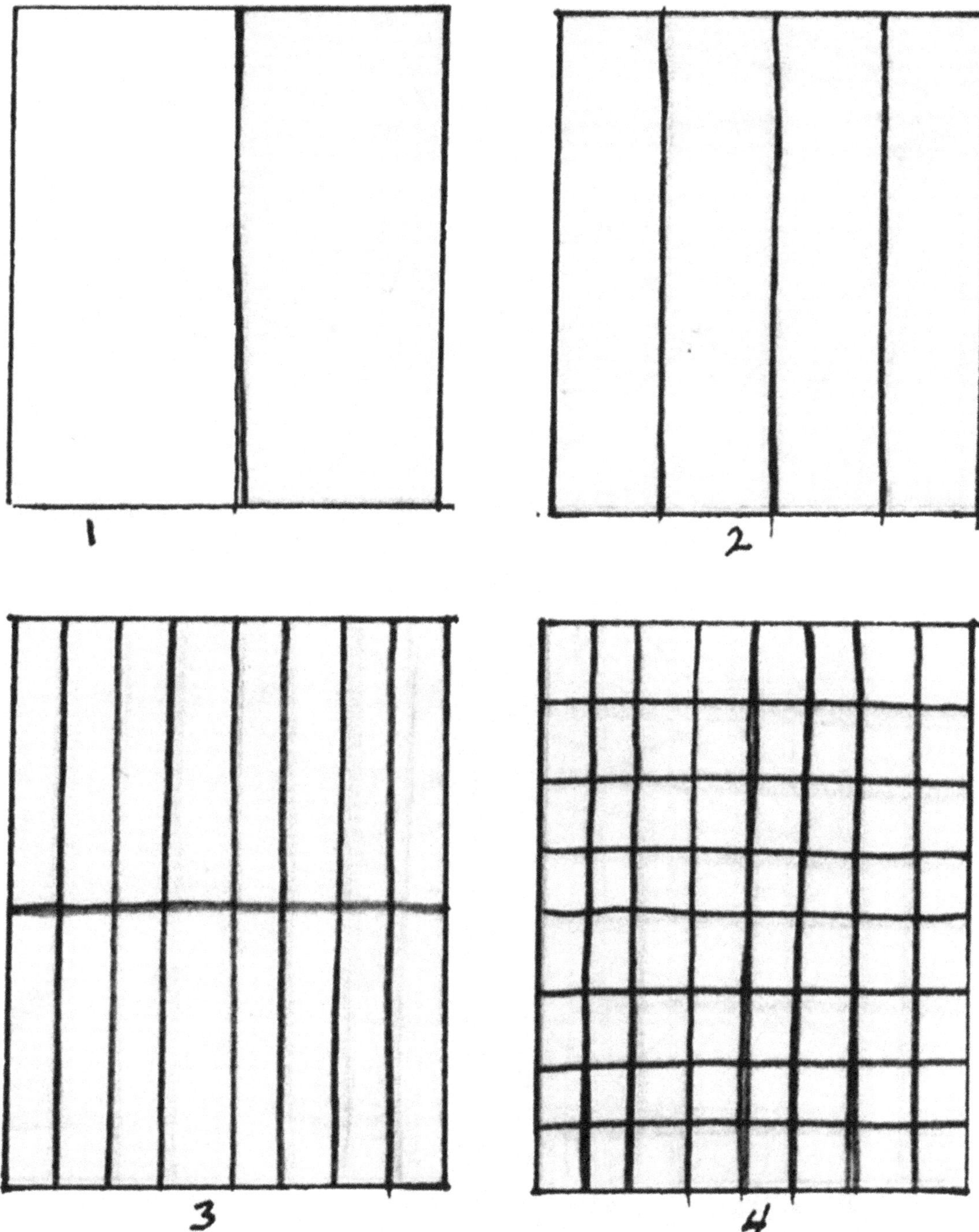

DIAGONAL PRACTICE:

a) Draw a diagonal line 1/3 down from the top
b) Draw a series of radiating lines across the page
c) Do the same from the opposite side and fill the page

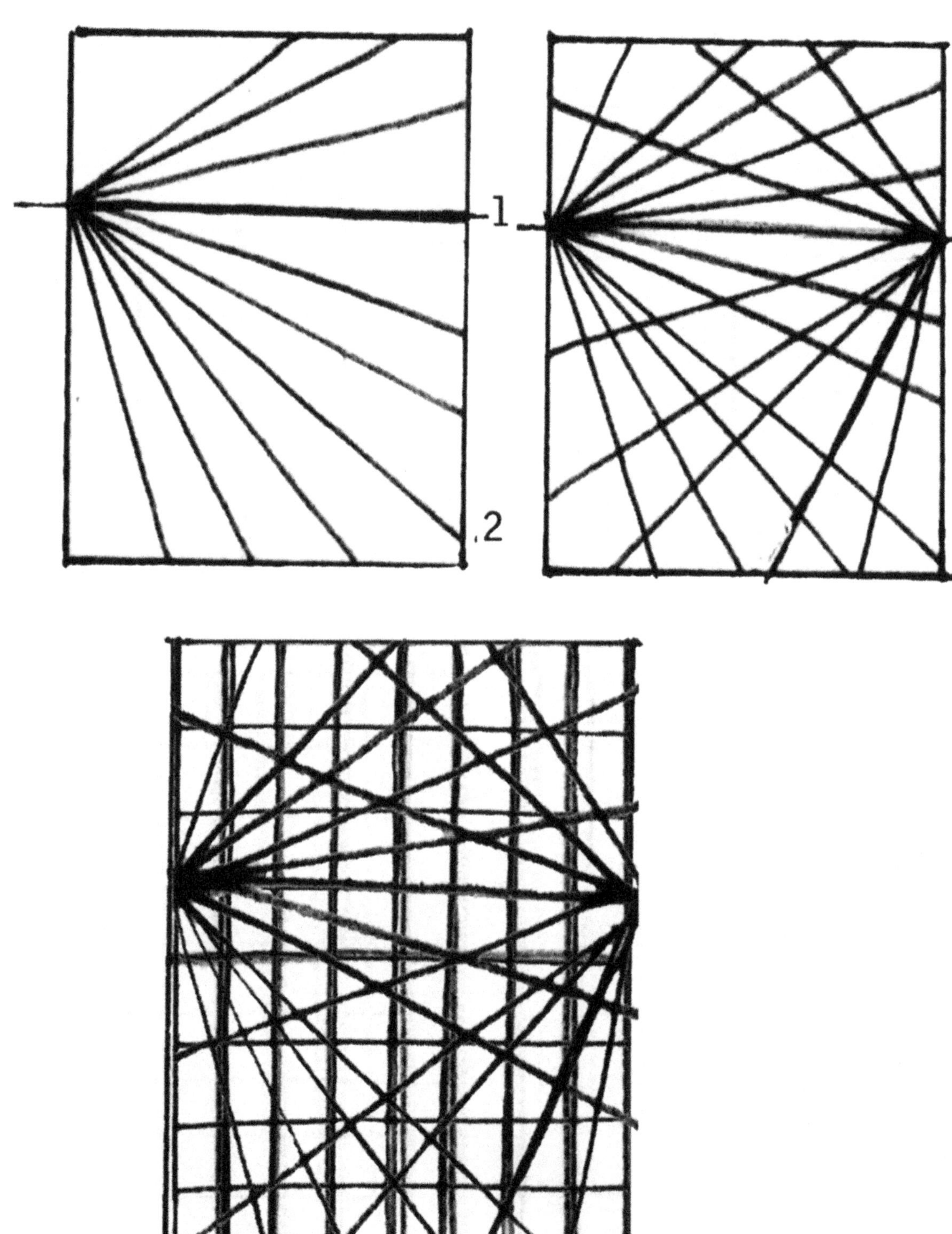

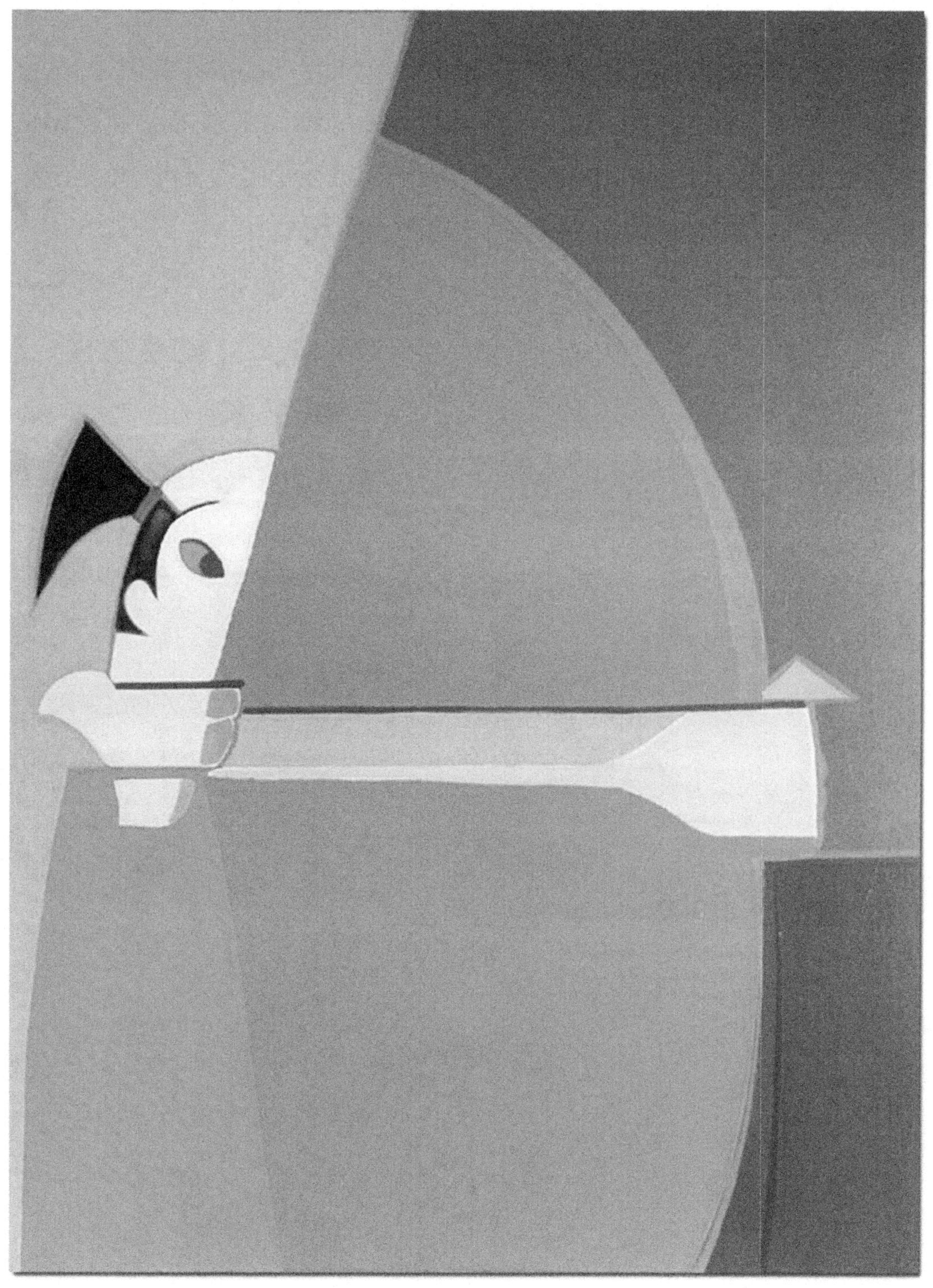

Archer, by Wayne Gilbert

The list of books in Section 3 presents different artists styles. Burne Hogarth's approach may seem suited to comics while George Bridgeman's work is a classical style. The beauty of their work is derived from the same source material - the human form.

Learn it and draw with confidence.

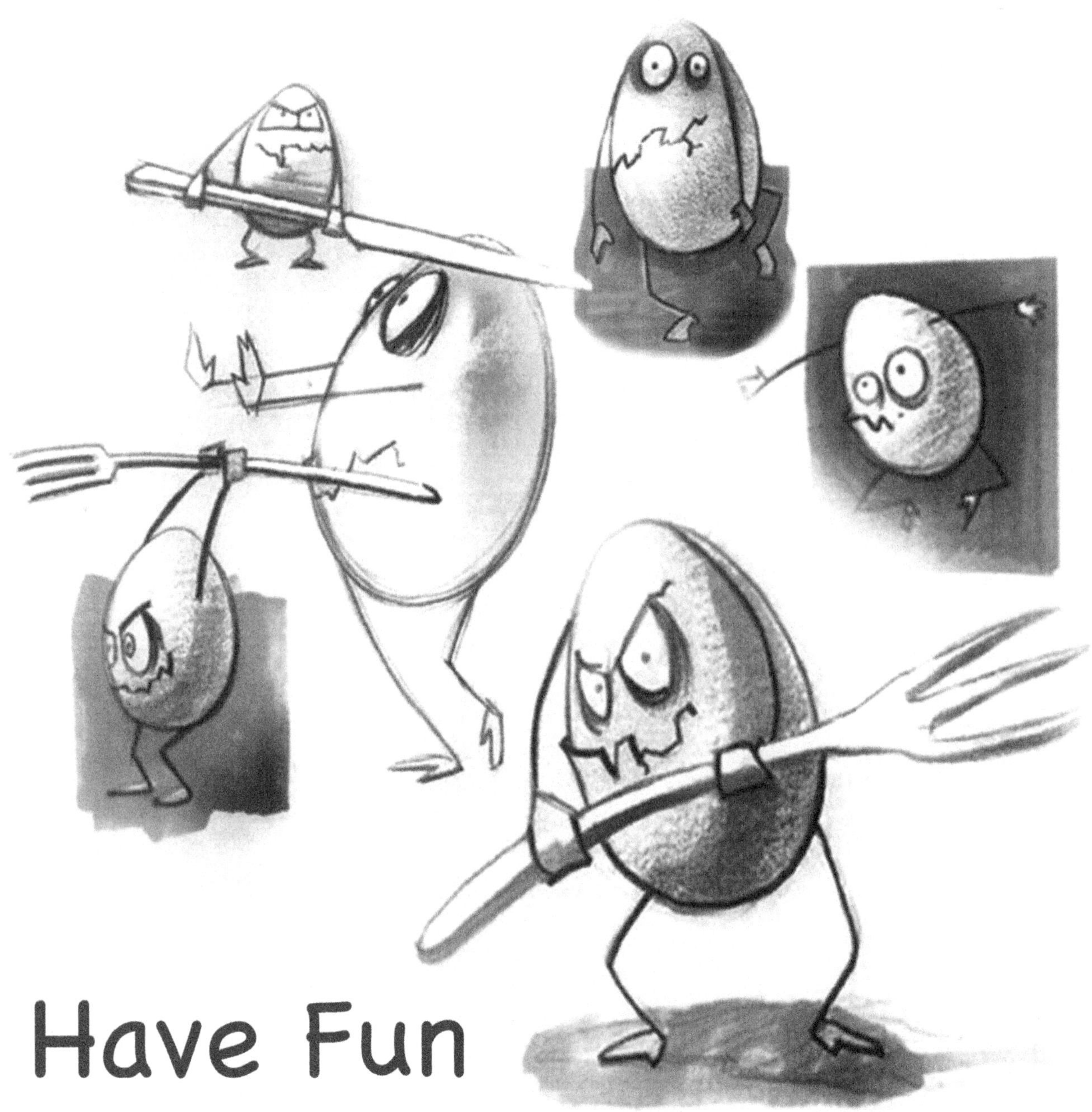

Have Fun

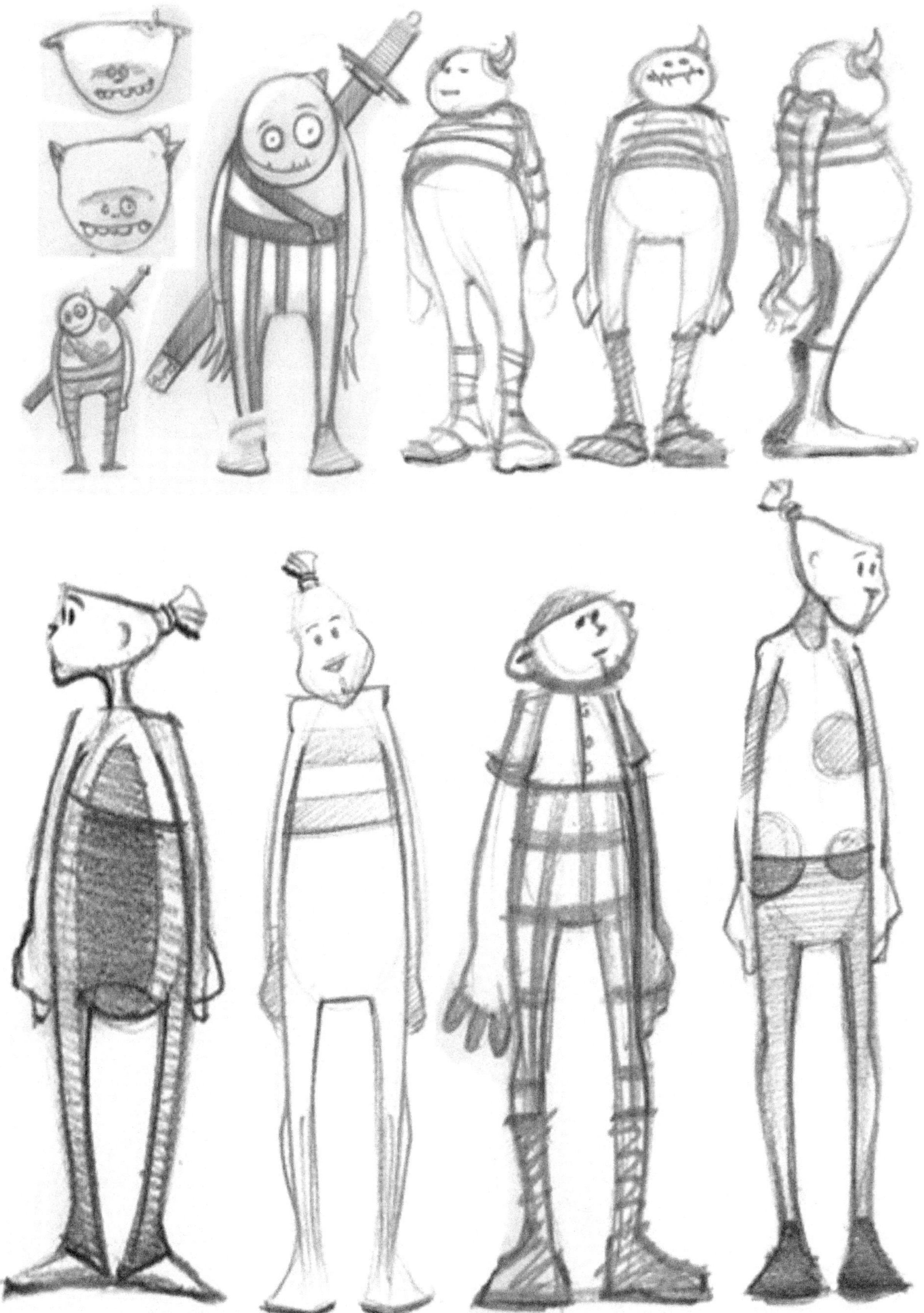

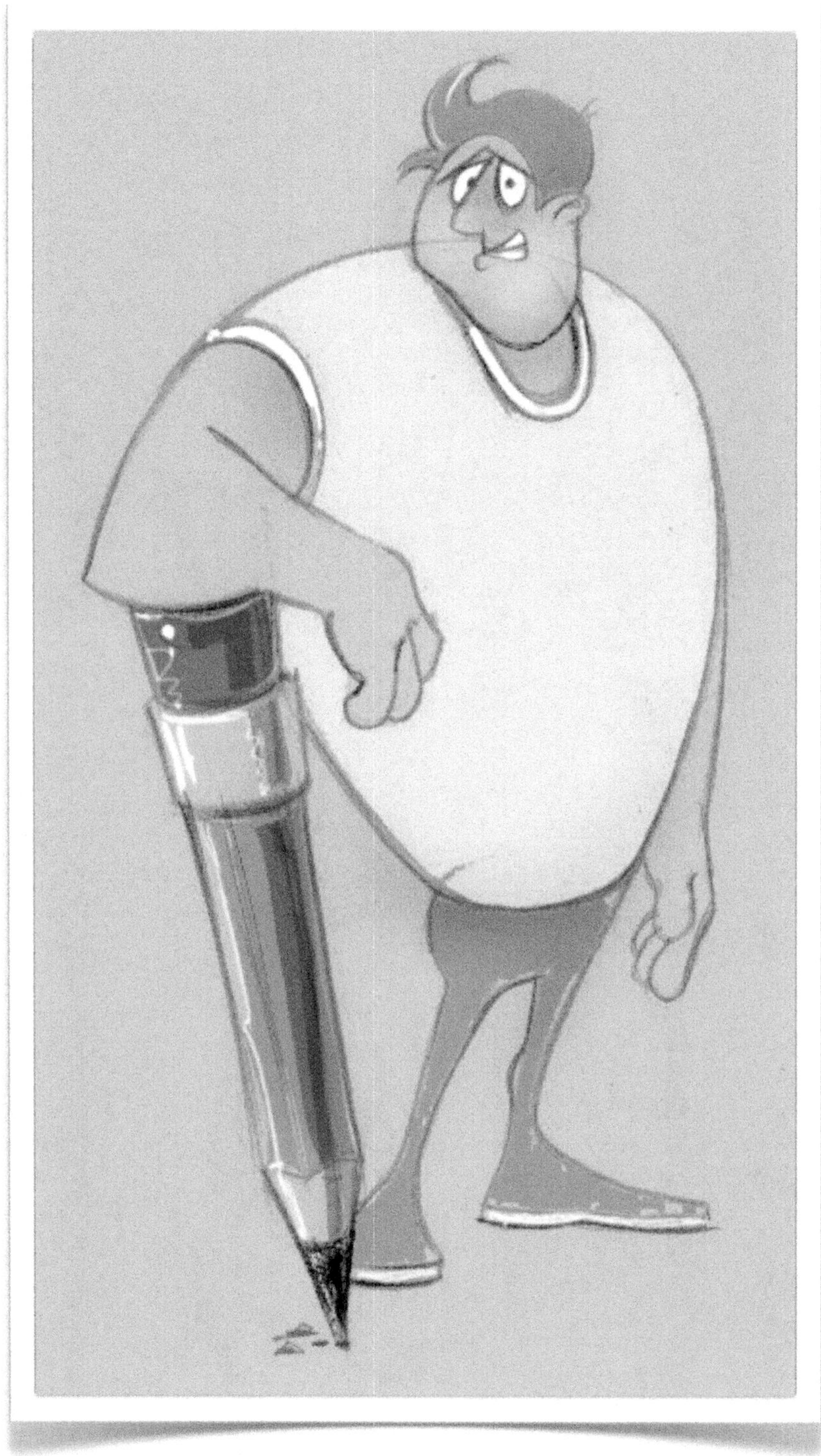

Now start here and go that way...

Made in the USA
Las Vegas, NV
30 January 2022

42602550R00057